The Humanistic Psychologist

| Volume 33 | Number 4 | 2005 |

Psychology Press
Taylor & Francis Group

New York London

SUBSCRIBER INFORMATION

The Humanistic Psychologist is published quarterly by Lawrence Erlbaum Associates, Inc., 10 Industrial Avenue, Mahwah, NJ 07430–2262. Subscriptions for 2005 are only available on a calendar-year basis.

Individual rates: Print Plus Online: $30.00 in US/Canada, $60.00 outside US/Canada. Institutional rates: Print-Only: $95.00 in US/Canada, $125.00 outside US/Canada. Online-Only: $90.00 in US/Canada and outside US/Canada. Print Plus Online: $100.00 in US/Canada, $130.00 outside US/Canada. Visit LEA's Web site at http://www.erlbaum.com to view a free sample.

Subscriptions to *The Humanistic Psychologist* are provided automatically to members of Division 32 of the American Psychological Association.

Order subscriptions through the Journal Subscription Department, Lawrence Erlbaum Associates, Inc., 10 Industrial Avenue, Mahwah, NJ 07430–2262.

Microform copies of this journal are available through ProQuest Information and Learning, P.O. Box 1346, Ann Arbor, MI 48106–1346. For more information, call 1-800-521-0600, x2888.

THE HUMANISTIC PSYCHOLOGIST, *33*(4), 249–251
Copyright © 2005, Lawrence Erlbaum Associates, Inc.

EDITOR'S INTRODUCTION

One of the things we thought about when we began making plans for the merger of *Methods* with *The Humanistic Psychologist* was whether to keep *Methods* as an annual issue that would appear as one of four regular issues of *The Humanistic Psychologist*, or whether to simply make research and methodology articles a part of *The Humanistic Psychologist* without focusing them into a single issue each year. The virtue of our decision to keep the identity of *Methods* posted on the cover of our annual methodology issue was to ensure that we would have at least one issue's worth of such articles each year. The very good news is that last year we had such an abundance of submissions that were relevant to research and therapeutic methodology, that we decided to go ahead with two *Methods* issues: Vol. 32, No. 2 produced by *The Humanistic Psychologist* Associate Editor Scott Churchill, and the Vol. 32, No. 4 "special issue" devoted to transpersonal research produced by Guest Editor Rosemarie Anderson.

The introduction to the Vol. 32, No. 2 issue was apparently lost en route to the printer, so I will simply review here the contributions to that issue. Russell Walsh discussed researcher reflexivity from a hermeneutic perspective; Gilbert Garza presented a didactic application of the "Duquesne" phenomenological method; David Smith reflected on methodological issues pertaining to the impact of theories and constructs in psychotherapeutic settings; and James Pappas presented his award winning paper from Division 32's 2003 Sidney M. Jourard Symposium, in which he discussed methodological issues in transpersonal research.

This issue begins with a short piece by the late Patton Howell. Pat was the "patron saint" of *Methods: A Journal for Human Science*—he was its founding editor (along with Don Polkinghorne), and served as dedicated publisher and financial underwriter from its inception in 1986 until the merger 2 years ago. Those who knew Pat will remember him as a kind and gentle soul, a champion of humanistic psychology and one of its finest proponents. Pat passed away in May, one week before his 84th birthday, as this issue was going to press. He was a dear friend and mentor to me; and, in memory of Pat, I include here as a prelude a piece he was working on, entitled "Healing Hatred," excerpted from work he had begun in the aftermath of 9/11.

This issue, in the spirit of the inaugural *The Humanistic Psychologist—Methods* (Vol. 31, No. 4), includes an archival piece, this time drawn from an early manuscript of the late Rolf von Eckartsberg. It is interesting to note that Ernest Keen (whose "Doing Psychology Phenomenologically" was published in the inaugural issue) and Rolf von Eckartsberg were at Harvard together in the early 1960s, studying under the tutelage of Gordon Allport and Timothy Leary (for whom Rolf served as graduate assistant from 1961–1963). Keen and von Eckartsberg each reflected their mentors' interests in their own work, demonstrating a sensitivity to the social context of research and to the more subtle dimensions of conscious experience in their personal choice of research topics.

One of the original Graduate Faculty in the program of existential–phenomenological psychology at Duquesne University, Rolf was an edifice within the department: a "rock foundation" from whom many students and colleagues found a source of nourishing support. His contribution went far beyond that of his intellectual advances in the fields of social psychology and hermeneutic phenomenology; he became a living example of his own philosophy of spiritually based conviviality and inspired fellowship. When studying the stream of consciousness in particular situations or during particular "timeflows," Rolf became fascinated by the social organization of the field of consciousness and the intersubjective constitution of what he called "landscapes of consciousness." He believed that human social living must be based on an ethical and spiritual value foundation: a transpersonal ground. It was Rolf's overall intention to develop an ecologically oriented field-theory of human existence conceived in terms of an interdependent network of conscious events and social relationships constituting an "existential village." Rolf's ever illuminating discursive exploration of the structures of conscious experiencing inspired his students to widen their own frames of reference and to see themselves, and each other, through new eyes.

Linda Finlay's contribution to this issue is an extension of her work in qualitative research methodology, this time reflecting on the theme of "reflexivity" that runs through much of her recent scholarship. Here she draws on the phenomenological literature on empathy and places it into dialogue with hermeneutic principles, using examples of her own research reflections as points of reference and highlighting how the intersubjective process of empathizing with participants is a fundamentally embodied experience. Her aim here is to articulate concretely what the researcher is experiencing when engaged in a lived, bodily reflection on qualitative data.

Edward Delgado-Romero and George Howard take up a humanistic critique of mainstream psychological research from an intriguing angle: one that uses meta-analysis and quantitative evaluation methodology to illuminate problems with several research literatures in psychology. The problems revealed by their analysis are argued to be a result of our discipline's preference for (statistically defined) "significant" rather than "nonsignificant" findings, with respect to what kinds of research get published in traditional journals. Bayesian statistics are proposed as an alternative whose more holistic (that is, less binary in terms of accepting vs. rejecting null hypotheses) approach could serve as a corrective to at least some of the problems inherent in natural science psychology.

In addition to the aforementioned methodologically oriented articles, there are two special inclusions. One is Larry Leitner's Presidential Address from the 110th Annual Convention in Chicago. We normally publish presidential addresses in the division journal, but Larry was hesitant to act as editor for his own address. Because he was in the process of an editorial review of the piece I was working on for a subsequent issue, we decided that I would act in turn as editor on his piece. Because our new publisher makes it possible for us to print more pages per issue than in the past, we have decided to include both of our articles here.

Please continue to send submissions as well as proposals or queries for the *Methods* issues to me via e-mail attachment at bonobo@udallas.edu or via hard copy at 1845 East Northgate Drive, Irving, TX 75062. I want to especially emphasize that I am interested in contributions from the wider membership of Division 32 as well as from colleagues who might not have submitted methodologically oriented work to a journal before. Reflection on what it is that we are doing when encountering our "data" is something that all of us are capable of producing. Beginners, as well as seasoned researchers, all have contributions to make in the ongoing effort of humanistic psychology to redefine itself in the new millennium.

Scott D. Churchill
Editor, *Methods* issues

THE HUMANISTIC PSYCHOLOGIST, *33*(4), 253–257

Healing Hatred

Patton Howell
President
Dallas Discussion Group

Many people get overwhelmed by anger because their emotions are entangled with abstract thoughts. Their anger becomes hatred of someone or something and finally turns to self-hatred. I have been conducting a practice to heal hate. This way of healing is successful when my clients can relive the realities of childhood.

CHILDREN'S THINKING

Each time adults use abstract thinking, there is less reality in their thinking, and finally none. They become trapped into rationalizing actions driven by emotions. Childhood realistic thinking can protect and disentangle rational thought from emotion. We can use emotions to clean out and tune up the body. Humans have survived when emotions have been guided by reality.

Children undergo their deepest mental development during the first 6 years of their life. At birth, a child's brain cells have the capacity to wire cells together. At about 1 year, the child has more neural connections ready to wire the brain than at any other time of life.

Children inherit, through their genes, empty connections between their cells. They are like blank lines on which they will write their experiences of reality. They have 6 years to use as many of these connections as they can. They are establishing the deep lasting structures, which will support their realistic thinking for the rest of their lives.

Correspondence should be addressed to Scott D. Churchill, 1845 East Northgate Drive, Irving, TX 75062. E-mail: bonobo@udallas.edu

At age 7, people begin to learn abstract thinking in school. It is a linear, one-dimensional language of cause and effect. Rules begin to control children's lives, rather than holistic reality. Unused connections disappear rapidly over the next 10 years, until they reach age 16. At that time, they will have about the same number of brain cell connections that they will have for the rest of their lives. These are the important years, years when children think realistically.

For practical purposes, realistic thinking begins at birth. The medium of education at this time is emotions. Infants respond to and initiate the emotions of love from their mother, unless the mother feels only hate, in which case the infant's emotion is hate.

The child can become calm and centered in reality or become unstable in emotions of hatred. In the first case, the child becomes more involved in reality. The resonance of moving light and colors harmonizes into pictures of reality. Touch becomes more than emotion. It becomes real. Sound condenses into patterns of reality. The child's world can be meaningfully expressed in structures of sight, sound, and touch.

Emotions such as anger and rage can find full expression within deep structures of holistic reality, but the emotion disappears after a few minutes. Abstract thinking is not yet available to make anger and rage into an addiction.

Infants imitate adults' expressions. At 1 year, they know perfectly well the spoken sound of "horse," even though they cannot say it yet. They love peek-a-boo and baby talk; as adults' voices rise to a higher tone, infants know the adults are talking to them and for them.

Children wire their brains by discriminating realities, such as the smell of their mother from the smell of other people. Experiments have shown that a picture of a familiar face from early childhood will cause one unique brain cell to make connections with many other cells. By 4 months, they know whom to trust and whom to fear. Also they know the reality of care, as opposed to neglect. Before they acquire language, they communicate with gestures—when an object is too far away, when milk is coming. These are the realities of their lives.

In their teens people seem to have given up the world of reality for the adult world of reason and abstract cause and effect. Sometimes they act realistically even though thinking the opposite in abstractions. Rationally teens decide to give up hate, but they do not give it up. Where is their free will, their freedom of choice? Their lives are turned upside down. But what if there is a will of reality that is stronger than rational abstract will—a will of hardly noticed vibrations, rhythms, and patterns of thought. Childhood reality is on the teenagers' side. It can heal hatred even though they do not realize it is happening.

Remember that the rhythms, tones, and patterns of realistic thoughts are the human reality. The body is animal. Emotions are not part of human reality. They are animal self. When one can disentangle oneself from emotion, one is ready to heal hatred.

"I AM A DOG"

My healing hate practice began 20 years ago, with a client who was flirting with hatred of the United States. She found her thinking sometimes got confused and ineffective when hatred overwhelmed her. I can see her gray eyes as dams tangled with hatred. This may have been the key I was looking for.

When her anger tangled with reason, its feeling shape often became a hot, transparent bubble enclosing her. She pushed on the fluid surfaces but remained a prisoner of her hate.

We did a meditation in which anger was its own reality. There was no target for the anger. She moved this anger up her spine from a center in her groin where blood began to pound; then to her abdomen which tensed up; then to her chest as breathing quickened and deepened, and her neck swelled; and then her head began to throb with blood flow and her eyes glistened with sharper focus. She acknowledged the emotional high of the anger and let it slowly absorb her body. Finally, it became so powerful that she let it out the top of her head. I told her I could see what must be a tongue of fire flickering over her head, and she laughed, feeling some liberation. She had not rationalized the anger onto someone else. It was just a simple reality of her body. I said,

> When a dog is angry the emotion lasts at best for 6 min, then the dog gets over it and goes about his business. The pure emotion of anger that you feel is the same as the dog's. You are both animals. Do you realize that by concentrating on physical reality you have delivered an anger that is a celebration of yourself rather than being caused by an abstract person?

She realized that emotion could clean her body out, tune it up. As we talked about the problem in the following weeks, it became clear that anger was actually very good for her body.

Several weeks passed. We tried again. This time there was not a rationalized hatred of the United States, but pure, wonderfully cleansing, animal anger. She could feel the difference between her emotions and her abstract thinking. She felt a sense of liberation.

She said, "Wonderful, I'm a dog." She was ready to use her emotions in a positive, creative way.

She was beginning to know the difference between hatred and cleansing anger. In a few months, she would manage to tune up her anger so that she was in charge, naturally balanced between physical anger and practical reality—keeping her rational thoughts at bay when she felt emotion.

Abstract thinking cannot disentangle itself from emotions. Think about when you are angry at someone. The emotion of anger does not last very long. You notice your anger is disappearing. What is happening? You are a dog. You need constant stimulation to keep the high of anger going. So you begin to rationalize your anger. "He should not have deliberately put me down in front of everyone." Now your anger returns, and you begin the cycle of rationalizing to produce more emotional highs again ... and again ... and again. Many people reside in such bubbles of hate for the rest of their lives.

HATRED CAN RUN THROUGH EVERYONE'S HEART

The possibility of self-hate resides in the heart of every human being. How can we control anger and hatred in ourselves? There are many ways. Here is my approach.

1. Identify emotions, childhood thinking, and abstract thinking.
2. Learn to enjoy the physical benefits of pure anger.
3. Move to social situations portrayed in the theater.
4. Try nonhate techniques in religion and Asian martial arts.
5. Identify the "enemy" technique of creating hatred of others to solidify political power.
6. Feel the self-confidence to try new ways to control anger leading to rage and hatred.

One can conquer and control self-hate with practical, realistic thought. It will give one the mental fuel needed to tune up and power one's thinking. One cannot merely tell someone not to hate. That is useless abstraction. Abstractions are like rules. They are not reality. Abstract thinking makes human society possible, but it also makes addiction to hatred possible. People can avoid the addiction when they learn to separate the ways they think.

My problem with this first step has been the daily practice of generating the pure emotion of anger without reference to anyone else. It is difficult to control anger when one is already tangled up in hatred.

If one has been exercising the pure emotion of anger daily, one is ready for the next step. A daughter of mine, who is an actress and teacher, told me about the theater art of anger and hate. First, an actor imagines the "character" whom he is supposed to hate and why he is going to hate him. The "character" is not the actor playing him. The performer is hating the character he has imagined. He really and freely hates the "character." When the play is over the beneficial effect of the emotion fades away in a moment and, bingo, there is no one to hate. The character was not the actor. The actor has just enjoyed emotion without hate. He is invigorated from the animal anger, and he is centered in peace.

The next time you are angry with someone, pretend that he is a character in a play. Later your emotion of anger will quietly die away instead of hardening into hate.

There are a number of Asian sports, such as Karate, which demand that one has no ill will for his opponent. If the practitioner fears and hates him, he will lose his rhythm and his edge.

Politics provides a nice example. A politician thinks he must unify a following by accusing an opponent of misdeeds that will cause the politician's followers to unite in hatred against his opponent. The opponent will do the same. Both will have caused useless hate. Can the country survive in the present day through hate in politics? It does not work.

If people choose to heal hatred in themselves, they can do it. Each person must make an individual choice and a commitment. In the last 30 years, the United States has moved from southern states with a racist bias to a tolerable society. This happened because individuals chose not to hate. It takes one person at a time.

ACKNOWLEDGMENTS

Patton Howell's wife Joan was gracious to allow us to publish this informal excerpt from his most recent writing.

AUTHOR NOTE

R. Patton Howell was born on May 23, 1921, and passed away on May 16, 2005. Dr. Howell was an Eagle Scout, a graduate of the Woodrow Wilson School of Public and International Affairs at Princeton University, and later in life earned a doctorate in psychophysiology from the Saybrook Institute. He had been a United Press Staff Correspondent, a teacher, and president of a consulting firm specializing in international affairs. At the time of his death, Dr. Howell was serving as founder and president of the Dallas Discussion Group. He was founder and past president of PEN Texas and the Isthmus Institute, as well as a trustee of the Saybrook Institute, the Isthmus Institute, and director of the Western Human Science Foundation. He wrote *Beyond Literacy: The Second Gutenberg Revolution* (W. W. Norton, New York, 1990), earning the Benjamin Franklin Award for best nonfiction literature in 1991. Dr. Howell had written or edited 11 books, including *War's End* (W.W. Norton, New York, 1989) and *Locked In To Life* (Tea Road Press, 2002). He also served as Nominator for the Nobel Prize Committee for Literature in 2001.

Methods: A Journal for Human Science was sustained by Dr. Howell's steadfast vision and unwavering support from its inception in 1986 to its merger with *The Humanistic Psychologist* in 2003.

THE HUMANISTIC PSYCHOLOGIST, *33*(4), 259–270

How Will I Proceed?— What Is My Method?

Rolf von Eckartsberg

Psychology Department
Duquesne University

I have become increasingly dissatisfied with the contemporary American psychological research literature, because it seldom shows me much of anything of relevance for the understanding of my own life or that of others, and, in particular, I rarely find any references to personal experiences. You can read most of the scientific psychological journals without ever learning anything about the experiences of the subjects themselves with whom the experiments were done and who ought to have some ideas about it.

Not only is the subject of psychological investigations rarely consulted about his experience and interpretation of what was going on, nor is he asked to tell us his own reasons for behaving as he did. Most frequently he is placed in highly artificial and contrived experimental situations and asked to perform unusual tasks referred to as "behavioral responses." What the subject does—his responses—psychologists then take as the data of their investigation. They are looking at the bodily behavior of somebody in a special context, and they record what the person bodily does as he interacts with that situation, more typically, as he responds to the changes in the situation initiated by the experimenter. What does this look like and how does it operate in a concrete laboratory situation? Let me tell you about an experience I once had in my undergraduate days in a psychological experiment.

Imagine yourself given the instructions that you are about to participate in a scientific research problem on the "psychology of people." The psychologist tells me this while we walk down into the basement dungeon of this building. He gives me a pat on the back and gently but firmly shoves me into a dark and completely bare cubicle-type room, maybe a seven-foot cube. I stand in front of a gadget that looks like a poor man's version of a vending machine. It is a big black-painted piece of

---

Correspondence should be addressed to Scott D. Churchill, 1845 East Northgate Drive, Irving, TX 75062. E-mail: bonobo@udallas.edu

plywood. In the middle there is a silver stick, like a handle, protruding and there is a silver tray beneath which looks like a money return cup where the peanuts come out in a vender. I sit down in the chair which was obviously placed there for my working convenience, because this is what I have come here for, to perform some work. That's how it is in my mind anyway. So I sit down and remember that he had told me something before; I was to push the lever back and forth—for what, I can't remember exactly. But to push the lever: *that* I remember. Oh, yes, he said I was to pull the lever as often as I wanted to. That struck me curious, "as often as I wanted to," as if I had anything to do with it. I was here to demonstrate some scientific principle; I knew that much, and he was setting it up so that I could. So here I was alone in this dark room about to pull the lever, which I then proceeded to do cooperatively. I start away and something comes rushing down "tzzsschuu-uuuuuuuckel" the chute and "cling": there in the silver cup tray is a piece of candy. I welcome it into this adventure and chew on it happily while I keep pulling the knob because I was told to and besides there really isn't much else to do here. After a while another candy tumbles down and pretty soon it becomes a game for me, because I have realized by now that there is some hidden order in this chaos, not to say madness—some rules by which my opponent plays. These candies stand in relationship to my pulling, obviously. What could the game be? I sit and ponder about the possibilities. I start counting the number of times I pull, lose count, and start again. I am going to figure out this system and beat it, I say to myself, and the task has become much more interesting. I try out various maneuvers. I think about them, try to evaluate them but it does not jell for me. I keep trying, varying the pulls from fast to slow, sometimes just plain getting tired in my arm. That is my reality as I sit in this booth. If I knew what was going on in the other room, if I knew what my imaginary game partner, the psychologist-researcher was actually doing and interested in I might not even be as moderately enthusiastic as I actually am now.

The experimenter, the man who made me do all these things was not at all interested in my experience, in my primary living reality, as I tried to figure out the system, how I felt frustrated, bemused and outright sullen or even angry at times at myself or the gadget or against the experimenter, my imaginary game partner. He could not care less as to what I experienced. All he is interested in is what I am doing, how many times and in what pattern I pulled the lever. And he is not even interested in this activity of mine in and of itself, but he is only interested in what I did in response to what he did, how he set up the environment-apparatus to control and guide my behavior. He wants to know about the relationship of my pulling the lever and the regularity—which he establishes—of the "goody" which comes tumbling down the shoot to me in a mysterious but challenging logical regularity. I never question that it must be logical, that is what you expect in an experiment.

So what I experience and ruminate about in the situation is deadwood for the experimenter, totally irrelevant. All he is interested in is the *amount of total bar-presses* or the *rate of pressing* in relationship to the *number of reinforcements*, that is what he calls the fact that the goodies come tumbling down and you pick them up and eat them or save them, whichever. They are the rewards, the *reinforcements*. In other words, the experimenter is not interested in me, primarily, as a unique person, or in what I go through in my experience. How could he be when he actually has a mechanical and electronic counter keeping track of my activities and automatically sets it to release the "goodies" for me as a function of my bar-presses? He thus need not even be bodily present to my ordeal while he is "running." He is interested in behavior and in *rates of response* and *schedules of reinforcement*. The experimenter is happy that I play his game and that my behavior is becoming shaped by his manipulation. It makes sense to me too trying to figure out the system and adapt my ways during the game to fit the situation better, whether I know what is going on or not. My body adapts itself to this situation quite intelligently to improve its performance. From my behavior the experimenter will come up with an impressive generalization about human behavior, about random-, variable-and-fixed-, "ratio" and "interval" *schedules of reinforcement* allegedly underlying the gambling activities and fabulous business success of Las Vegas, Nevada. This conceptualization is also supposedly accounting for the experience I would have as a tourist locked in mortal combat with a one-arm bandit who is heisting me while I am trying to jackroll "him" in the gambling parlor. He has also devoured many of my dimes, stolen my attention, sweat and honor as a combatant but shown only frustrating-payoff-stinginess, and that only very sporadically, which, nevertheless, by its very unpredictability and shameless cheating intrigues me to keep at it longer and more persistently than it is wise for me and my purse. Random ratio-interval schedules of reinforcement are the most persistent because they are unpredictable. They keep you on your toes, trying. It would get dull if I knew that I got one goodie for every tenth lever-pull, although I would perhaps keep working if I liked the goodies. However, if I knew the system and didn't like the payoff, I would change to something more interesting. But then the experimenter would lose his control and hold over me, his artificial environment would not shape my behavior any more and he would not like this.

The point of my argument is that I, as the subject in the experiment, as actor, do experience much myself while undergoing the routine of "being run as a subject." But this, my own living reality which is very obvious and the most meaningful aspect of my living then and there, is ignored by the experimenter, while my muscular performance, my "behavior" is carefully attended to. This makes it understandable why he might just as well study rats or pigeons to get the same results. He does not have to worry about their experience. They could not talk back even if they wanted to and they are docile and easy to manage, keep and "sacrifice" when they have done their job for science.

It seems to me that all the arguments which say that we must start with molecular units and slowly build up a science that fits also human behavior are fallacious and even fraudulent. If I study animals I arrive an animal-psychology. If I treat humans as I would animals in a Skinner box, that still does not make it *human psychology*. It is a psychology of humans limited to their animal-behavioral-level.[1] I think that if we leave out the essential human dimension of experience, we do not have a fully human psychology. The realm of experience is the domain of subjectively lived reality which is all the reality I, the acting subject, have. I do not think it is legitimate to ignore that reality and to deal exclusively with externally observable behavioral responses emitted under stimulus control. It is only a normal scientific prejudice which declares that only stimulus-response units are to be considered objective and real. Psychology certainly has to deal with *human reality* and that is primarily *experienced reality*.

I can see, though, why psychology in its behavioral camp has gone the way it has. It is based on a thorough going belief in material determinism. Any phenomenon is interpreted in the direction of its antecedent physiological condition. All human realities are linked to their bodily manifestation, to behavior and psychology, and my experience of being anxious, cooped up in a tiny cubicle, is considered to be my physiological-endocrine response to a certain pattern of visual stimuli. But as soon as they jump to this new reductive level of explanation, behaviorists forget that they have left out a crucial aspect: human experience. If they succeed in their technology of environmental determinism, if they can predict what I will do in their constructed restrictive setting, if they can "control" my behavior, they claim that this is the way humans act all the time. I think that this is a one-sided view. I do not deny that there is much *environmental determinism* and that we often act under *stimulus control*, but I maintain that this is primarily the case where I am not aware of what is going on, as described in the experiment above. As soon as I know what the constellation of the environment is, as soon as I become aware of its meaning and structure, I then gain freedom to choose to continue acting the way I have or to stop. I am under stimulus-control as long as I decide to cooperate with the experimenter and his instructions. If I realize what schedule of reinforcement I am on, if I know the payoff conditions, I can utilize this knowledge and integrate it into my own planning. I thus bring the situation under my own control rather than let the situation control me.

In real-life-settings, the determinants of my actions are multiple and complex. There is so much stimulation going on and hitting my body from all sides and way beyond the range of my attentive awareness. Now it is with regard to these

---

[1] Editor's note: In an issue of *The American Psychologist* (October 1998, *53*, p. 10) devoted to Edward Thorndike's animal psychology, Stan and Kalmanovitch (p. 1135) countered Thorndike's criticism of "anthropomorphism" in animal psychology with the incipient "theriomorphism" and "mechanicomorphism" inherent in Thorndike's work (where theriomorphism is the reduction of the human to the animal level of functioning, and mechanicomorphism is the reduction of animal functioning to that of a machine); the combined "mechanicotheriomorphism" seems a much more dangerous threat to human and animal psychology than the "anthropomorphism" that has concerned animal psychologists over the years.

out-of-awareness "inputs" that I am in the same situation as I would be in a behaviorist Skinner box: These inputs determine me rather than I them. But much of the situation is also thematic for me. I attend to it consciously. Let me say that I am scanning the room for a familiar face or that I am looking for a hammer. These activities are definitely *not* determined from the outside—except in the most general sense that they are existentially situation-bound—but they originate in my intention to look or to use the hammer. To "originate" here means that they take their origin within me, they arise as possibilities in my awareness.

It is thus only with regard to situations in which I cooperate with the experimenter to follow his procedures and manipulations and to "play his game" that the model of laboratory psychology works. It is not invalid but inadequate. It yields scientific results and conclusions that are valid and useful. But what are they useful for? It seems to me that they are useful in that they allow me to make predictions about the behavior of people and actually to control their behavior if I have total central control over their situation or the selection of situations. By means of reinforcements I can shape behavior, this is true. However, this procedure has certain presuppositions which are not much talked about.

First, in order for the scientific experiment to work I must have complete control of the situation which very significantly includes the willingness of the subject to cooperate with me in the first place. Most subjects readily agree to cooperate considering it as their humble contribution to the divinity of science revealed in the laboratory situation. They must want to do it and I as the experimenter must also assume that they will be honest and natural. In other words, I expect them to do what they would normally and naturally in such circumstances.

Secondly, I must make the task interesting so that the subject is motivated to perform as well and as honestly as he can or I appeal to him to make an effort and help me out, for science's sake. I give him a pay-off that interests him because he likes it (we call that "positive reinforcement") or because it is painful to him such as an electric shock which I allow the subject to avoid if he is smart and does the right thing (we call that "negative reinforcement"). In both cases the subject will respond and give me a chance to shape his behavior further.

Thirdly, in order to obtain "pure reactions" scientists usually cut out all extraneous diversions (Straus, 1963). They put subjects in a harness or in a sensorially deprived environment in which only those things are present and prominent to which the experimenter wants them to attend, such as the lever in the Skinner box described before. In such an approach I may gain precision and control over parameters but I also lose human relevance. I will never forget my first fantasy (or would you call it reaction?) in a demonstration experiment using a Skinner box. I could not understand what was so great about it because these ideas immediately rushed to my attention: "No wonder it works, what else is there to do. This is completely unlike any natural environment I know. It is thoroughly restricted, contrived, manipulated and inhuman." I could even say that it is so for animals because the rats in my own basement enjoy an infinitely more interesting setting than those poor docile white Norwegian rats in this cage. None of the experiments contrived in the laboratory really do justice to the rats' intelligence. In such a setting, I, or any animal, am merely a puppet being led around and controlled by the master-manipulator. When I later read Skinner's *Walden II* it did not help much, if any, to change my mind. I believe that if I create an artificial environment and if I then observe people in such an environment I will always get somewhat artificial results depending on the nature of the environment and behavior that I study. Natural situations have always been more attractive to me as possibilities for studying human psychology.

Naturally, I do get useful results from psychological laboratory procedures. As I said before, I will be able to make predictions about behavior, given similar circumstances. But I can also arrive at actuarial predictions from natural situations as well, as the ecologists and insurance men well know. Their predictions have direct human relevance. So why not start with spontaneously occurring natural behavior, and, moreover, why not focus on the behavior of individuals and consult them as to their concomitant experience? *That is the least I can do if I claim to be a human psychologist.*

My major concern is as follows: I know that environmental control works, and it works better the less I, the subject, know about what is going on. That is, the more the influences work directly on my body out-of-awareness. I am indeed influenced and shaped by my environment. This is a fact and a reality which nobody can deny. We are beginning to realize the extent of this more and more as we increasingly create and dwell in man-made artifactual environments—take the spacecraft as its most perfected prototype in which literally everything, even the air, is completely controlled—that they have their unequivocal functions built right into them, thus limiting the possibilities of human creative variation. However, I must say in all fairness, that these specialized environments also allow the functioning of specialized human possibilities to occur which would otherwise not exist. Take television (to be discussed in some detail in a later chapter) as an example. We are simultaneously limited and freed by television. All artifacts serve as extensions of human functions. We adapt to them. Thus it is clear that:

My Environment Shapes Me

But we have to become aware and be wary. Instead of further increasing the control over our behavior, which is the agonizing ongoing trend, I believe we should rather begin to study seriously the effect of these environmental influences on our own experiences. For instance, what does it mean, and what is it like to live in a spacecraft, or being bombarded by television, being locked-in and hooked-up with a machine for long periods of time? It is not enough to study related physiological functions. We must also know about these effects in psychological-experimental terms.

This is the level at which their pervasive effect will become manifest, in your and in my experience, in my enjoyment perhaps also in my suffering.

The major paradox lies in the fact that environments can run me or I can run my environment. This is basically an inextricable relationship, a situation of *interpenetration*. I always live in situations, and these situations provide limited opportunities. But besides the environmental determination there is the environment-utilization and that, to me, indicates a situation of freedom and of responsible awareness regarding the forces operating on me. I must learn about the possibilities of situations and increase my discrimination, understanding, and skill *vis a vis* environments.

I Become Liberated From Environmental Determination Through Understanding

This learning is personal-experiential-learning. You and I must begin to experience possibilities in situations as a preliminary for personal autonomy and responsible action. The attempt to study my experienced activities in situations poses serious problems. While external behavior, as observed, i.e., physical-space-time-movement, can be recorded objectively, the study of experience is dependent upon self-observation and verbal report, in short: *self-expression*. In order to learn about my experience I must become subjective, "introspective," and I must become able to put into language what I find myself experiencing. Natural scientists have raised serious objections against the validity and objectivity of such "subjective reports," and they generally do not want to become involved with them. I believe that such avoidance of the dimension of experience in psychology is a serious problem and appalling deficiency in contemporary American psychology.

Because I propose to write about *experiential psychology* I must clarify what methods I am using in arriving at my statements. In the widest sense I am using the method of "self report," and I lean heavily on the insights and studies of phenomenologists (Strasser, 1963; Van Kaam, 1966). They, as far as I can see, try to programmatically study human experience from a descriptive-point-of-view. As I perceive the world in front of, around, and within me, I can try to describe what I experience. I can pay attention to anything that occurs in my consciousness and try to describe it as accurately and in as much detail as possible. This includes a manifold of processes or activities which have been traditionally differentiated into the categories of perceptual process, feelings and thought processes, into "outer" and "inner perceptions." However, these levels or "domains of experience" have to be clearly defined and differentiated whether it can be sensation, perception, memory, anticipations, fantasy, feelings, planning, daydreams, thinking, judging, evaluating or what have you. Some of these activities are directed toward the *"world-pole of experience,"* as in perception, some more oriented toward the *"self-pole"* such as feeling, and others are in between, such as daydreaming. But let me leave the attempt to describe and differentiate several interconnected domains of consciousness until later. All that matters here is to emphasize that all consciousness is directed toward something, that is, always there is something given in consciousness in some fashion. Phenomenologists call this basic characteristic of consciousness *"intentionality."*

All Consciousness is Intentional

Consciousness is intentional, it is pointing toward something. It is even connecting me with the things of which I am conscious.

All Consciousness is Connecting

This means that consciousness always has a direction or an orientation toward an object. This basic character is best understood in the case of human perception. When I see, I always see something, a tree, a house, a person, a landscape. This is how the natural world presents itself to me: I perceive it in some aspect, given to my eyes, ears, touch, taste or smell. Something is given physically to my body-flesh in its differentiated sensory modalities.

Consciousness Is Presence To Reality

Through consciousness I become present to and connected with the world. This is really a quite obvious observation that consciousness is always connective and hence "of something," that is, that consciousness is intending something, connecting me with something. However, this insight regarding human conscious experience has great consequences. It means that also in my thoughts, memories, daydreams, and even probably in my feelings there is something given to my attention. Something presents itself in a certain fashion and it depends on the realm of consciousness that I momentarily focus on and dwell in, whether in thought or memory, daydream, etc., as to how it is presented. This characteristic of consciousness that it occurs on different levels, in different domains, I want to indicate by way of an analogy. Let me speak of *landscapes*. I know that there are different landscapes in the world of physical reality such as mountains, deserts, polar icecap, valleys, etc., that there are natural visual landscapes, microscopic landscapes, auditory landscapes, the landscape of smell, etc. In other words, it is useful to speak of the natural orderings in consciousness that I can identify with some practice, of the realm of perception, of memory, of daydream, of thinking as different *landscapes* to which I can attend in consciousness, in which I can dwell and move. I am not talking here about single objects of consciousness such as this tree, but of natural groupings, stylistically proximate and continuous realms of consciousness, such as a forest-landscape would be in perception. Landscapes are situations in which I find myself, experiential situations. In human experience we have the power to attend to, live in, or in some form or other to be connected with different "experiential landscapes."

Consciousness Is Dwelling And Moving
In Experiential Landscapes

Awake body-sensory-perception, because of its vividness and the immediateness of our bodily involvement as well as the tangible nature of our connectedness with our perceptual world, has a privileged position in the hierarchy of domains of consciousness. Through my bodily-sensory-perceptual-involvement I enjoy a primordial and original participation in the world of daily life. As contrasted to the primordial-perceptual-landscapes all other realms of consciousness seem modifications, derivations, transformations. My awareness connects me with my world in its manifold dimensions or landscapes—both outside with the tangible world as well as inside with my worlds of imagination—and in awareness I move within these landscapes. Just as the perceptual landscape is there concretely in front of me in tangible connection, so are the "inner landscapes" of memory, thinking, etc., *there*, in front of me, within me, "before my mind's eye," though not in a tangible connection but in a "connection of awareness," of pointing-reference, of meaning, in image, idea, concept. This means that on any level of consciousness I am dealing with objects given to my awareness explicitly or implicitly, whether an actual tree, my memory of this tree, the concept "tree," or a fantasy involving trees. My task, as an "experiential psychologist," is to describe the different ways in which these objects are present to me and the different ways in which I am connected with these objects, in which I am meeting and dealing with these objects. Also, I must study and determine what the objects of my consciousness are. I must work out differential criteria for distinguishing levels or landscapes of consciousness, their relationship to one another and my modes of involvement in them.

The task can be approached through self-experience-observation and self-experience-description. I consider this to be a perfectly respectable scientific procedure which when communicated and thus objectified as data can be independently verified by other researchers. I would even go further than this and start to consider literary works as legitimate experiential data for scientific analysis. One can look at writers as experts or professionals in the domain of experience, both in experiencing itself but also in the expression of experience. Very few average naïve subjects will be able to articulate their experience sufficiently to provide good specimen-records. The usual sampling procedures of psychology, therefore, have to be re-examined from the point of view of an experiential psychology.

How can I proceed with self-observation? There are essentially two ways both of which are traditionally called "reflection."

Self-Observation Proceeds Through Reflection

Some phenomenologists maintain that I can reflect on my experience only once it is passed, that is *retrospectively* by calling an event into my attention as memory, while others say that I can train myself to become even more attentive and present to my own stream of experience while it is going on. The latter view implies a belief in the human possibility to work for and develop increasing self-awareness which can be rendered public through description. I favor this latter position.

In the following I wish to proceed along this line of investigation by considering "awareness" to be the "thematic consciousness of events or happenings in the flux of ongoing experience." The validity and fertility of experiential psychological studies conceived on this model will depend on the personal training and ability of the researcher or his collaborators to make discriminating self-observations, to articulate and thus to communicate these experiences in a language-form understandable to others. I consider my book to be an initial and limited attempt in this direction based on and elaborating the pioneering work of many phenomenologists and other scholars, friends, and acquaintances who have taught me what I know.

Through systematic descriptive efforts we may, some day, arrive at the possibility of mapping the stream of awareness. I want to call this endeavor:

Ecology of Human Consciousness

The methodological difficulties of this enterprise to record the stream of consciousness as an effort in the "ecology of consciousness" are tremendous. While it is relatively easy to record physical-space-time-movements from a behavioral ecological observer point of view, how can I achieve a similar kind of reliable inter-subjective and verifiable running record of experiential events?

The principle of indeterminacy which states that I necessarily influence and change the phenomena that I am studying by studying them, applies forcefully here. While it also occurs but is more subtle in the laboratory where it hides in the laboratory setting itself, it is blatant in these pages. As I write I dwell in my gaze on the surface of the paper. This wakens almost automatically in me the non-sensory-perceptual landscapes of my experience, the "what-I-think-and-write about-." In order to describe what I see with my eyes I have to go back and forth between looking at this thing and then writing it down, a complicated form of translation. It would perhaps be methodologically purer if I were to dictate my experiences into a tape recorder, because speech is not as closely tied to vision as is writing. I am trying it out to dictate my experiences into a tape-recorder but find it difficult. The noise of my own voice is too harsh for the more meditative silence of visual observation; the loudness of my speech startles me and destroys the subtle bonds of immediate beholding. Vocalized speech is for people from one to another which has a different energy level, not the soft vibrations of silent self-experience-observation but the awakening body-quake of the resonant loudness of being addressed by another. Besides, I feel funny talking to myself aloud though I am a pretty good self-conversationalist in the silent wrestling of thinking. Often my thinking dictates itself in formed silent speech, in structured logical language. I have command over this language—it is a ready-made descriptive-precision-instrument at my disposal, ready to be case in a thousand different operations and to do its enveloping and pointing task in all directions and on all levels.

So I have to stay mostly with the written language as my medium of discourse with myself and with you.

Language Is A Miracle Of Versatility

Language serves as a "universal register" to quote the phenomenologist Kwant, in terms of which all levels and areas of human experience can be expressed and related to one another.

Language Is Universal Mediator

I think that I realize what some of the important methodological problems are, inherent in my endeavor. There is the fact that the use of language already implies necessarily some interpretation and that it represents a clear translation of one lived reality into another, the transposition of reality of experiencing.

Speaking is subjective and cultural at the same time. Speech creates a new reality, the shared reality of discourse which is inter-subjective and even "objective" by being written down while the lived experiential reality that speech represents, is much more volatile and forever elusive and temporary. We cannot do without records or data and the written language—or the tape—are just as much and validly "data" as are bar-press-responses. However, my written report on my own private-subjective-experience is more complicated and subject to more contingent influences than a simple muscular reflex in response to some induced stimulation. But such is the nature of experience; it is very complex, subtle, and elusive. That is the point of my argument

REFERENCES

Strasser, S. (1963). *Phenomenology and the human sciences.* Pittsburgh: Duquesne University Press.
Straus, E. (1963) *The primary world of the senses.* New York: Free Press of Glencoe, Illinois.
Van Kaam, A. (1966) *Existential foundations of psychology.* Pittsburgh: Duquesne University Press.

ACKNOWLEDGMENTS

This chapter was written in the 1960s and is both a phenomenologist's critique of the traditional psychological experiment and a prolegomena to a new form of psychological research. This text was the second chapter of an unpublished book-length manuscript entitled Conscious Living: Explorations in Ecstatic Experience, c. 1967 found by the Editor among the late Rolf von Eckartsberg's personal writings. Elsa von Eckartsberg graciously allowed this second chapter from the larger work to be excerpted here. The book was to be a comprehensive introduction to Rolf's early development of a social psychology, inspired to some extent by the Dissertation he completed at Harvard University under the mentorship of Gordon Allport. This article was slightly edited for publication by Scott Churchill.

THE HUMANISTIC PSYCHOLOGIST, *33*(4), 271–292

"Reflexive Embodied Empathy": A Phenomenology of Participant–Researcher Intersubjectivity

Linda Finlay

Faculty of Social Sciences
Open University

In this article, I advocate a research process that involves engaging, reflexively, with the embodied intersubjective relationship researchers have with participants. I call this practice *reflexive embodied empathy*. First, I explicate the concept of empathy through exploring ideas from the philosophical phenomenological literature. I then apply this theory to practice and offer examples of reflexive analysis of embodied empathy taken from various hermeneutic phenomenological research projects. Three interpenetrating layers of reflexivity are described, each involving different but coexisting dimensions of embodied intersubjectivity. The 1st layer—*connecting-of*—demonstrates how people can tune into another's bodily way of being through using their own embodied reactions. The 2nd layer—*acting-into*—focuses on empathy as imaginative self-transposal and calls attention to the way existences (beings) are intertwined in a dynamic of doubling and mirroring. The 3rd layer—*merging-with*—involves a "reciprocal insertion and intertwining" of others in oneself and of one in them (Merleau-Ponty, 1964/1968, p. 138), where self-understanding and other-understanding unite in mutual transformation. Through different examples of reflexive analysis from my research, I have tried to show how intersubjective corporeal commonality enables the possibility of empathy and how, in turn, empathy enables understanding of the Other and self-understanding. I discuss how the coexisting layers of empathy and the resultant understandings can be enabled through hermeneutic reflection and collaborative research methods.

"The body is the vehicle of being in the world," said Merleau-Ponty (1945/1962, p 82). More than this, the body is the vehicle for understanding the world, he ar-

---

Correspondence should be addressed to Linda Finlay, 29 Blenheim Terrace, Scarborough, North Yorkshire, United Kingdom, YO12 7HD. E-mail: L.H.Finlay@open.ac.uk

gued. It is through an individual's own embodied consciousness that an understanding of the Other is gained. In his later work, Merleau-Ponty (1964/1968) elaborated this idea to argue for 'incorporeal being,' an intersubjective intertwining. Using the metaphor of the chiasm—criss-crossing—he suggested that a kind of corporeal reflexivity is the foundation on which self-reflection and personal identity rests.

Applying Merleau-Ponty's (1945/1962) ideas of embodiment, understanding, and self-reflection to the phenomenological research process, I argue that empathy is not just about emotional knowing, it is a felt, embodied, intersubjective experience. It is also an experience that underpins researchers' ability to understand their participants. For this reason, these researchers need to learn to read and interrogate their body's response to, and relationship with, the body of the research participant (the Other). First, as a psychologist studies a person's life world, that person's sense of embodiment is a significant existential dimension that requires the psychologist's fullest attention. Researchers need to try to grasp something of the Other as a "living, lived body." Second, they also should attend to their own bodies as researchers—specifically the body that is in relationship with the participant. I am therefore advocating a research process that involves engaging, reflexively, with the participant's lived body, the researcher's own body, and the researcher's embodied intersubjective relationship with the participant. I call this practice *reflexive embodied empathy.*

To define and explicate this concept, I start by exploring some of the literature on empathy. There is an extensive empirical literature on empathy in the fields of neuroscience (see Thompson, 2001) and social psychology (see Davis, 1994). However, I confine my discussion here to the equally extensive (though sometimes overlooked) literature from phenomenology. Here, I draw on a range of theoretical ideas, but the philosophical ideas of Husserl (1952/1989) on intersubjectivity and of Merleau-Ponty (1964/1968) on "embodiment as intertwining" are particularly influential. Although the focus in this literature review is on empathy, concepts related to embodiment and reflexivity are integral.

The literature review is followed by an analysis of the concept of reflexive embodied empathy in practice. I use three examples of significant moments from various hermeneutic phenomenological research projects to demonstrate reflexive analysis of my own embodied, intersubjective relationships with participants. I characterize these moments of reflective involvement with the data as fluid, interpermeating "layers" whereby different dimensions of experience are called to the fore. Three coexisting layers of reflexivity are described:

- *connecting-of* the Other's embodiment to our own,
- *acting-into* the Other's bodily experience, and
- *merging-with* the Other's bodily experience.

A discussion section develops this layered understanding of reflexive embodied empathy. There is a fluid movement from using one's own experience as a way of understanding another's embodiment to exploring the relational intersubjective empathic space between participant and researcher where self-understanding and other-understanding are intertwined. The implications of this for the practice of reflexivity in research are explored and elaborated.

PHENOMENOLOGICAL CONCEPTIONS OF EMPATHY

Defining Empathy

The term *empathy* is the English translation of the German term *Einfühlung,* which means "feeling into," or gently sensing another person or an object in the process of trying to appreciate it. In 1897, Lipps introduced the concept of *Einfühlung* into his writing on aesthetics:

> An observer is stimulated by the sight of an object ... soon the observer feels himself into the object, loses consciousness of himself, and experiences the object as if his own identity had disappeared ... The observer sees a mountain ... As his gaze moves upward to the peak of the mountain, his own neck muscles tense and for the moment there is a sensation of rising. (Lipps, cited in Peloquin, 1995, p. 25)

When this idea is applied to the human world, empathy is generally understood as entering another's world. Carl Rogers (1975) offered the benchmark definition:

> It means entering the private world of the other and becoming thoroughly at home in it. It involves being sensitive, moment to moment, to the changing felt meanings which flow in this other person. ... It means temporarily living in his/her life, moving about in it delicately without making judgements ... as you look with fresh and unfrightened eyes." (Rogers, 1975, p. 3)

Empathy in these terms is linked to the Rogerian counseling technique of reflecting back clients' meanings. Done well, it involves much more than simply repeating clients' words and empathetically representing what has been said. Instead, it is a relational process. Empathy here involves being a safe and steady human presence, being one who is willing to be with the client, whatever comes up. When clients go into therapy, usually they are able to articulate only a little of their troubles; much more is felt and sensed in what can be called an embodied and "more-than-verbal" way (Gendlin, 1981). Through their attempt to reflect back what clients seem to be saying and meaning (not arguing or shifting agendas), therapists go with their clients precisely to the spot at which this inner more-than-verbal space is opening. Todres (1990) picked up this point when he described four modalities of *being with*, arguing that these demonstrate the intersubjective foundation of psychotherapy.

O'Hara (1997) also argued for a relational empathy, although her concern was to focus on sociocentric, rather than Western egocentric, understandings. Empathy, she argued, needs to be understood as "an essential feature of human, relational connectedness, an expansion of a person's consciousness to include in their perceptual field the other as an individual and the relationship with the other which he or she is a part" (O'Hara, 1997, p. 313). Levin (1988) also drew on these transpersonal themes, viewing empathy as, in part, a form of "transpersonal identification." Referring to Whitman's poem, "Song of Myself," he explained:

> What he is describing are experiences of bonding, of cross-identification, experiences in which his identity is inseparably intertwined with the other, and in which, to an extent, he *becomes* the other. His own separate identity is transcended; although remaining "himself," he feels "inside" the other, lives in, and inhabits, the other. (Levin, 1988, p. 299)

Levin (1988) went on to argue that if one's identity is intertwined with that of others, there is hope that, through compassion, humanity can build a new society based on cultivating, learning, and teaching this reciprocal sociality:

> The transpersonal fulfillment of our initial, prepersonally organized intercorporeality is not a confusion of identities, but rather a deeply felt compassion—an openness and readiness to be *moved* by compassion—and an uncompromising respect for the other *as* other, the other *as* different, but for whose difference one is capable, nonetheless, of feeling some bodily grounded sympathy (Levin, 1988, p. 301).

Explicating the Experience of Empathy

If people understand empathy as openness, presence and relational interconnectivity, how can they make sense of the process taking place at this moment?

This question has been explored by a number of phenomenological philosophers. Stein's (1916/1989) doctoral dissertation, 'On the problem of empathy' (which she produced as Husserl's assistant and under his direction), is particularly notable. Following Husserl's work in *Ideas I*,[1] Stein, explicated empathy as a unique and irreducible kind of intentional experience. When one combines embodied sense perception and cognitive inference, she argued, one experiences another person as a unified whole through empathy. Pursuing this idea, she critiqued previous conceptions of empathy, which had a narrower focus. She described em-

---

[1]From the German original of 1913, originally titled *Ideas Pertaining to a Pure Phenomenology and to a Phenomenological Philosophy*, First Book. Newly translated with the full title by Fred Kersten. Dordrecht and Boston: Kluwer Academie Publishers, 1983. Known as *Ideas I*.

pathy as the experience of feeling led by an experience beyond oneself, and goes on to delineate how this is enacted through different modalities of accomplishment. First, the experience of the Other emerges before a person: "it arises before me all at once, it faces me as an object (such as the sadness I "read in another's face)" (1916/1989, p.10). Then, one imaginatively puts oneself in the place of the Other—reproducing the form of their experience in my own imagination. Finally, as the Other's experience has been clarified, the experience faces the person again in a richer, fully explicated way. Stein describes these levels as: "(1) the emergence of the experience, (2) the fulfilling explication, and (3) the comprehensive objectification of the explained experience" (1916/1989, p.10).

In tandem with Stein (1916/1989), Husserl (1952/1989) developed these ideas of empathy in his exploration of intersubjectivity—a topic he revisited several times over his career (notably in *Ideas II*). Husserl was concerned not so much with particular understanding of others but with the transcendental conditions that make possible such understanding. Specifically, he sought to know the "aesthesiological layer" of the Other: how one comes to apprehend the Other's body as a "lived body"—an understanding that is empathy. His argument is that intersubjectivity (cosubjectivity) is present prior to one's concrete perceptual encounter with another, and that it is intersubjectivity which allows empathy.

Husserl (1952/1989) saw empathy as constitutive of the other and as the condition of possible knowledge of an existing outer world. Through experiencing an Other's experience of the world (through empathy), one sees the world from outside one's own subjectivity and can then experience that world as objective and real: "the objective world, *depends* upon the transcendence of foreign subjectivity" (Husserl, 1959, cited in Zahavi, 2001, p.159). Without the Other, one cannot properly know who one is, and one cannot understand that the world is larger than one's experience of it. As Husserl presented it, the constitution of true transcendence occurs through empathy.

> All Objectivity, in this sense, is related back constitutively to what does not belong to the Ego proper, to the other-than-my-Ego's-own in the form, 'someone else'—that is to say: the non-Ego in the form, 'another Ego' (Husserl, 1974, cited in Zahavi, 2001, p.159).

Husserl (1952/1989) then offered some more concrete advice about how to gain an experience of an Other through the meditation of empathy. He suggested that individuals need to imaginatively transpose themselves to the other's place to follow them.

> I secure [the person's] motivations by placing myself in his situation, [with] his level of education, his development as a youth, etc., and to do so *I must needs share in that situation*; I not only empathize with his thinking, his feeling, and his action, but I must also *follow* him in them, his motives becoming my quasi-motives, ones which,

however, *motivate with insight* in the mode of intuitively fulfilling empathy (Husserl, 1952/1989, cited in Davidson, 2003, p. 121).

Importantly, the intersubjective process Husserl described is understood to involve an entirely embodied relationship. "In order to establish a mutual relationship between myself and an other, in order to communicate something to him, a Bodily relation ... must be instituted ... In empathy I participate in the other's positing" (Husserl, 1928/1989, p. 176–7).

Merleau-Ponty (1945/1962) elaborated this emphasis on the body, arguing that it is a human's corporeal commonality specifically that enables the possibility of real empathy. As he reminded, "it is precisely my body which perceives the body of another person" (Merleau-Ponty, 1945/1962, p. 354). Later, in *The Visible and the Invisible* (1964/1968) he radicalized this idea to focus on the intersubjective intertwining, which he described as "The intertwining of my life with the lives of others, of my body with the visible things, the intersection of my perceptual field with that of others" (p. 49). Here, Merleau-Ponty (1964/1968) called people's attention to the way existences (beings) are intertwined in a dynamic of doubling and mirroring. In a passage that encapsulates this recognition of reflexivity he stated that

> The mirror's ghost lies outside my body, and by the same token my own body's "invisibility" can invest the other bodies I see. Hence my body can assume segments derived from the body of another, just as my substance passes into them; man is the mirror for man (Merleau-Ponty, 1961/1964a, cited in Churchill, 2000–2001, pp. 29–30).

Thompson (2005), drawing on Husserl (1952/1989) and in collaboration with Depraz (2001), takes these ideas further by presenting a typology of empathy. As he sees it, empathy involves

1. The involuntary coupling or pairing of my living body with your living body in perception and action.
2. The imaginary movement or transposition of myself into your place.
3. The interpretation of you as an Other to me and of me as an Other to you.
4. The ethical and moral perception of you as a person" (Thompson, 2005, p. 5)

Thompson (2005) insisted that these four kinds of empathy are not separate. Instead, they occur together in face-to-face intersubjective experience. In the following passage, Thompson emphasized that the role of empathy is to be mutually constitutive through the intersubjective relationship:

> They intertwine through the lived body and through language. You imagine yourself in my place on the basis of the expressive similarity of our lived bodies. This experience of yours helps constitute me for myself, for I experience myself as an intersubjective being by empathetically grasping your empathetic experience of me. Con-

versely, I imagine myself in your place, and this experience of mine helps constitute you for yourself. As we communicate in language and gesture, we interpret and understand each other dialogically. (Thompson, 2005, p. 11)

EMBODIED EMPATHY APPLIED IN RESEARCH

Halling and Goldfarb (1991) explained that there is a need to take embodiment seriously during the research process. Specifically, they argued, researchers should be aware of how they are being affected at a bodily level:

> To take embodiment seriously is to take seriously how one speaks and how one listens to self and other. The recognition that one is an embodied being includes the acknowledgement that even in a situation of being an observer one is an involved observer—someone who is being affected by and is affecting what is taking place. Being a researcher ... requires that one become fully and thoughtfully involved. It is as if one is engaged in a dance of moving forward and moving back: one steps closer and steps away, has an effect and is affected, all as an embodied being. (1991, p. 328)

More than just being aware of embodiment, researchers need to attend to the intersubjective relationship between participant and researcher. As Burns (2003, p. 232) pointed out, a researcher's own "embodied subjectivity interacts with that of the respondent in the mutual construction of meanings/bodies ... no 'body' can exist neutrally outside this process of inter-corporeality or inter-subjectivity." She advocated a critical embodied reflexivity that involves construction, deconstruction, and reconstruction of embodied subjectivities, thus providing rich material for analysis.

The theoretical literature outlined in the previous section identifies empathy as the basis of our sociality, our intersubjectivity and our capacity to understand an Other. Although descriptions of empathy come mainly from the fields of psychotherapy and philosophy, they seem to have applicability to psychological research. Here, the researcher's task is not simply to listen to another's story: the researcher also needs to be open to being with the participant in a relationship. The researcher needs awareness of how the bodily relationship between participant and researcher is mutually constitutive. The researcher's capacity to understand can be enhanced through this reflexive awareness.

Although the philosophical literature on empathy is rich and compelling, the question of how this coconstituting empathy might be applied in actual research practice has been less well explored. However, Churchill (2003), Davidson (1975), and Spiegelberg (1998, 2000/2001, 2003), among others, offered some valuable guidance. Drawing on phenomenological philosophy, Churchill, Lowery, McNally, and Rao (1998) recommend an intuitive "empathic dwelling" (p. 65) as the first stage of a phenomenological method. As Husserl said, "A first step is explicitly to be vitally at one with the other person in the intuitive understanding of his experiencing" (1936/1970, p. 328).

In this initial stage, the researcher aims to stay with the participant's description, becoming ever more open to what is being communicated. The empathic dwelling in this instance is enacted alongside the *epoche,* where the researcher attempts to put aside his or her own understandings to see the world anew. In empathy, "I participate in the other's positioning himself or herself from a unique perspective within a situation … While maintaining one's own position as researcher, one gradually allows oneself to feel one's way into the other's experience" (Churchill et al., 1998, p. 66).

Davidson (2003) explained that there are no short cuts for the cultivation of such empathic, intuitive understanding; it requires practice, skill, talent, and grace. Empathy, he said, is "a highly disciplined and demanding posture involving an active and artful use of all of one's faculties of memory, imagination, sensitivity, and awareness in coming to understand another person's experience from his or her own perspective" (p. 121). He drew a loose analogy of an actor learning to assume the role of a new character, and suggested that researchers might use similar techniques toward building imaginative bridges between their own and participants' experiences. A specific technique, for instance, might be for the researcher to recall a similar incident in their own life, and use that experience to help them to empathize.

Spiegelberg (1975) similarly argued that empathizing is not simply about putting oneself in the other's shoes. Instead, one has to leave behind one's own context and understandings to imaginatively project oneself into the Other's situation in an attempt to see the world through their eyes. Following Husserl (1952/1989), he called this process *imaginative self-transposal* (Depraz, 2001). Here, one spontaneously transposes oneself imaginatively into the Other. One hears another's joy that the Other has fallen in love and feels the Other's joy—transposing the Other as a possibility for oneself. One recalls a time in one's own life when the one had felt something similar and, providing one stays focused on the Other's experience and not one's own, one is able to feel empathy.

Yet how does this process of imaginative transposal come about in practice? When Husserl (1966, cited by Depraz, 2001) discussed this concept (*sich Hineinphantasieren*), he suggested that it is through an imagined kinaesthetic bodily exchanging that one is able to identify with the Other's psychic state. This stage is highly embodied as it relies on a "concretely dynamical spatializing of imagining." It seems researchers need to tune into this embodied and imaginative dimension as they feel into and with the Other.

EXAMPLES OF "REFLEXIVE EMBODIED EMPATHY" IN RESEARCH PRACTICE

In this section, I attempt to describe coexisting and interpermeating layers of empathy. Drawing on various phenomenological research projects I have been involved with, I focus on different examples—moments—of reflexive embodied empathy. The analytical extracts offered are based on notes taken from the reflexive diary I keep when I engage in phenomenological work. Using such extracts offers me the opportunity to engage in a process of *hermeneutic reflection* (Finlay, 2003a). Here the researcher's critical self-reflective involvement with the data allows different facets of the phenomenon to present themselves. Following Gadamer (1989), hermeneutic reflection can be understood as a process of continually reflecting on one's experience as a researcher, alongside the phenomenon being studied, so as to move beyond the partiality and investments of one's previous understandings.

Layer 1—Connecting of the Other's Embodiment to One's Own

People could not sense the physical qualities of the world unless they, too, were physical: that is, having the capacity to touch and be touched by the world. Similarly, people cannot grasp the intentional meanings of another's gestures if they are not capable of gestural intertwining with the Other. "He who sees cannot possess the visible unless he is possessed by it, unless he *is of it*" (Merleau-Ponty, 1964/1968, pp. 134–135). One's ability to move into the Other's bodily experience is predicated on one's experience of one's own body. One can "do empathy" because the Other is different from and like oneself.

The first example shows how empathetic understanding of an Other's experience of embodiment is intimately connected to the lived experience of the researcher's own. Here my reactions as an asthmatic in the presence of a patient dying from a lung disease helped me understand how the therapist I am observing is reacting in similarly personal ways to other patients:

> On one occasion during some participant observation research, I was observing an occupational therapist work with a client who was suffering from the final stages of lung cancer. Although I was supposed to only observe, I found I could not stop myself becoming involved (by asking the patient questions and even intervening at a practical level). When I reflected on my behavior, I understood it was my active need to be involved—to do something. I also recognized my own sensitivity as an asthmatic, witnessing someone with breathing problems dying of a lung disease. As I stayed with this patient I could feel my body resonate. I became aware my chest felt tight and I had to remind myself to breathe. Once I tuned into these bodily responses, I was then able to recognize my identification with the patient. I remembered my own struggles for life and being near death.

> Once I recognized these bodily responses, I was better able to see the bodily responses of the therapist. I could then see she was experiencing similar identifications with some of her other patients. Previously I had interpreted the therapist as being involved with fairly superficial, "irrelevant" tasks—now I could see these tasks had a

meaning for her: they were as much for her as the patient. *By examining my own embodied responses I could better understand hers.*

In my embodied experience, "I discover in that other body a miraculous prolongation of my own intentions ... As the parts of my body together comprise one system, so my body and the other person's are one whole, two sides of one and the same phenomenon, and the anonymous existence of which my body is the ever-renewed trace henceforth inhabits both bodies simultaneously" (1945/1962, p. 354).

This example shows at least two things. First, it suggests that to understand something in another, one needs to link it to something familiar to oneself—Stein's notion of identification. "In order to understand a movement, for example, a gesture of pride, I must first 'link' it to other similar movements familiar to me" (Stein 1916/1989, p. 59). Second, the example reveals how the world (more specifically, the Other) discloses itself through one's own bodily subjectivity. "It is as if the other person's intention inhabited my body" (Merleau-Ponty, 1945/1962, p. 185).

Probing our own embodied responses thus potentially opens up rich understandings of our participants. This kind of self-understanding (grounded in the Other's self-presentation) translates into Other-understanding. However, in this translation of using oneself to understand the Other, a critical question is raised: To what extent does one need to be the same as the Other to empathize? Stein (1916/1989) grappled with just this point. She noted that empathy can be successful when she looked at men's and children's hands and, although they were different from hers, she could see them as a "type": "I can only empathize with physical bodies of this type; only them can I interpret as living bodies" (p. 59). Even then, she argued, empathy is not limited to human physical body types, as people can empathize—through projection—with an injured animal. (I am reminded here of Paul Gallico's short novel (1970) of Jennie, which is a beautiful exploration of the physically embodied world of the cat.) However, there is a limit here, as certain bodily positions and movements cannot be empathized with. They are "empty presentations without the possibility of fulfillment. And the further I deviate from the type 'human being' the smaller does the number of possibilities of fulfillment become" (Stein, 1916/1989, p. 59). When there is too big a difference, the possibility of empathy is compromised. However, to some extent, differences can be transcended through empathy as one imaginatively identifies with the Other's position.

The process of imaginatively transposing oneself into an Other is highlighted in the next example. Here my attention shifted more towards the Other as the process of identification was sustained: this is Husserl's (1952/1989) notion of the Other being made "copresent" as analogue or mirroring of my Self.

Layer 2—Acting Into the Other's Bodily Experience

Merleau-Ponty (1945/1962) explained that to experience a structure is "not to receive it into oneself passively: it is to live it, to take it up, *assume it* [emphasis added] and discover its immanent significance" (p. 258). Understanding, therefore, comes from somehow taking up, identifying with, and then enacting the Other's experience. As Merleau-Ponty (1945/1962) said, "I have only the trace of a consciousness which evades me in its actuality and, when my gaze meets another gaze, *I re-enact the alien existence in a sort of reflection* [emphasis added]" (p. 352).

This notion of reenacting is reminiscent of Dilthey's (1927/1977) idea from his essay on "Understanding other people and their expressions of life" (Churchill, 2000–2001, p. 29). Dilthey described how higher forms of understanding consists of *"sich Hineinversetzen"* (meaning a projecting of oneself into the Other) and *"nacherleben"* (meaning reexperiencing or reenacting another's expressions and experience to understand them). According to Dilthey (1927/1977), to reexperience another's experience one needs to use one's imagination to "strengthen or weaken ... feelings, strivings, and lines of thought which are contained in our own context-of-life" (p. 133). It is necessary to shift attention from self to Other.

The next example shows this process of empathy through reexperiencing and reenacting the Other's experience. It comes from a group phenomenological study (Finlay et al., forthcoming) that explored, via an in-depth interview, the phenomenon of "mistrust" as perceived by 1 participant: Kath. Kath had the experience of being mistrusted by her colleagues, and as a result she felt herself to be attacked by others. She described finding herself becoming a different person—a "ghost" of herself: "I became a different kind of me, a lesser me." In the following extract from my reflexive diary, I reflect on Kath's changing sense of embodiment:

> I was struck by the way Kath seemed to have lost the embodied way-of-being she had previously relied upon. Having once been vivacious, bright, open, dynamic, and humorous, she was describing the experience of "pulling herself in" and becoming quiet and wary. Where once she had felt herself to be a "big" person—in terms of both her presence and her personality—she was now made to feel "reduced". In the process of being forced to reduce, she had become a different person. This is how she describes the process:
>
> Kath: It was this kind of shift and change and the pulling in and the unsafeness of that environment which before had felt secure, clearly wasn't. I was shaky. Lots of the sort of firm things that you believed in were now shaky. Does that make sense?
> Linda: Yes, so, when you say "pulling in" you pulled yourself into yourself
> Kath: Yes, I withdrew ...
> Linda: It seems like your very way of being is kind of quite open [mmm, mmm] and direct ... And here you've lost even your way of being.

Kath: ... that really sums it up actually. I felt the person who left that college was not me. Or was a paler shade of me ... I had to kind of slow down in a sense, not in speed sense but in a kinda closure sense ... in a protective sense.

As Kath was speaking, I was very aware of her "big presence." I had previously known Kath as a "big personality" and as someone who physically embodied a big, attractive presence. Yet, in the course of our interview, she somehow started to "fade" in front of my very eyes. I could feel a strange sensation within myself, a sense of closing down, closing in, shrinking, trying to become smaller, trying to become a "paler" version of myself. *Slowly I was disappearing. Then I realized that, strangely enough, this new reality actually felt safer. If I couldn't be seen, I wouldn't be hurt ...* I dwelt there some more ... I could understand and accept Kath's need to "reduce" and close down. At the same time, I began to feel something else. *Losing myself also felt slightly scary. Who would I be and who would I become if I was to disappear to be replaced by a paler-shaded me? I became aware that I felt somehow sad at the loss of my customary embodied way of being.* I looked at Kath and she, too, seemed to me to be sad and a little lost—indeed, vulnerable in her loss.

As I was listening to Kath, it seemed that what I was feeling was, in some sense, mirroring something in her. I rode with this idea. If this was the case, one way into understanding Kath's experience was to try to understand what was happening within me—or, more specifically, within and to *my* body. With this in mind, during the interview, I shared with Kath what was happening to me. I was aware that this could have had the unfortunate result of redirecting the focus from Kath to me. However, as it happened, I don't feel that what occurred detracted from Kath's experience. Instead, I believe that my attempt to empathize seemed to help her better articulate the pain of being a big woman forced to "reduce."

In this example, I show how I momentarily "transposed" myself into Kath's body. The process involved an act of creativity as I imagined what it would be like to live in her body—a body that was, in reality, quite a bit bigger than my own.

A crucial question is raised: To what extent was this imagining my imagining— my invention—as opposed to potentially reflecting something about Kath herself? Was this imagining simply projective distortion or a moment of genuine identification? This epistemological question is, of course, a critical point of debate for phenomenology. Phenomenologists of a more realist persuasion might be inclined to suggest that if the phenomenology was done well (e.g., effectively performing the *epoche*), then it should reveal that which is part of the phenomenon itself—in this case, something about mistrust. Those of a more postmodern relativist persuasion would argue that the idiographic findings are contingent on my style as researcher and my relationship with Kath. Another researcher would have obtained a different story (Finlay et al., forthcoming). I am poised somewhere between these two poles. I acknowledge the partial and tentative nature of the findings, but at the same time I believe that, through empathy, I have glimpsed something of Kath's perceptions and life world. In the process, however, I may not necessarily have glimpsed any essential structures of the phenomenon of mistrust at a general, as opposed to idiographic, level.

This raises the question of whether individuals can, in fact, ever know anything. No one—whether researcher or participant—has privileged access to the reality of human lived experience. When a participant narrates an experience in an interview, or a researcher provides a reflexive account, they offer an interpretation that seems to work at that time. The researcher then has to reflect on the evidence, recognizing its nonconclusive nature, and try to work with the participant. It was for this reason that I checked out my perceptions with Kath. I shared with her what was happening to me. Her response of "that sums it up" suggested that I had mirrored something of her experience. "As a mirror ... I re-enact the Other's existence by vesting in the Other's stance, gesture, expression a lived understanding of human intentions that *is* my presence to the world" (Churchill, 2000–2001, p. 30).

The idea of "reflection as reversibility" is developed further in the final example.

Layer 3—Merging With the Other's Bodily Experience

A key idea developed by Merleau-Ponty (1964/1968) is that the toucher and the touched are of the same material—the same flesh. He used the example of the touching hand being touched in part as a metaphor for the way body and world are intertwined. "The body-world boundary is a porous one, permitting of unceasing interpenetrability" (Aanstoos, 1991, p. 95). There is, in short, a merging-with.

This layer of empathy is shown in the next example, where I was analyzing an excerpt from an interview with a mental health therapist, Jenny. Jenny had been threatened by a male patient who had a violent sexual history. She described, at some length, her sense of apprehension that one predatory patient would eventually get her.

> Jenny: He's. ... extremely creepy. He will come up, want to touch you. ... He's a bit predatory in that he will follow you down corridors. ... He preyed across the gym ... crept up behind me. ... "They [colleagues] can't watch all of you all the time. ... I'll get you." ... He even does things like, there's a large observation window, and even if he can't physically get to you, he'll stand there and rub his groin and drool. ... He'll crawl across the floor to get you."
>
> In my analysis of this interview, I found myself reading and rereading the transcript with a growing sense of foreboding in the pit of my stomach. In the process of hermeneutic reflection, I started to imagine how I would feel in Jenny's shoes, stalked by this predator. What I experienced was literally an embodied reaction. Here is an extract from my reflexive diary, which reveals something of this reaction:
>
> Suddenly, the world begins to look different. Everything closes round me and somehow grows darker. I can hear the hollow beating of my heart. I think about the unit Jenny works in, seeing it now in terms of the spaces that are safe versus danger-

ous. She has to walk down public corridors all the time with full awareness she is not "safe." I feel her fear, that sense of menace where time is no defense. I experience her loathing, her disgust—my skin creeps in response to his creepiness. I see this same image of a man drooling and clawing at the window to get at me—it won't go away. It feels real, like it has happened to me. It is as if I have become Jenny.

This is the moment I wait for in my phenomenological analysis: the moment where I am so immersed in the data and intertwined with my participant I can no longer separate the pieces. Jenny's feeling of being stalked and bodily threatened by this creepy patient is also my feeling.

This example shows how I, as researcher, became so thoroughly immersed in my participant's experience that I (momentarily) lost sight of my own. Merleau-Ponty's (1960/1964b) words poetically described this strange experience I had of merging as researcher–participant: "to the extent that I understand, I no longer know who is speaking and who is listening" (p. 97)

Explaining the process of merging, Merleau-Ponty (1964/1968) used the metaphors of flesh (an ontological concept naming the elemental impermeability of our bodily inherence in the field of Being as a whole) and the chiasm (the crisscrossing of body and world). "We are the world that thinks itself—or the world is at the heart of our flesh" (Merleau-Ponty, 1964/1968, p. 136). Through carnal intersubjectivity "flesh meets flesh in the flesh of the world, and man can now become a living mirror for his fellow [sic] man" (McCleary, 1960/1964, p. 97).

With the intertwining, people "function as one unique body" (Merleau-Ponty, 1964/1968, p. 215). The meeting with the Other is a "chiasm" in which people are "two opennesses" (Merleau-Ponty, 1964/1968, p. 213) and in this crisscrossing a new intercorporeal being can emerge. The world is at the heart of the flesh; the flesh of the world and oneself as flesh are intertwined. The world and the individual are within one another (Merleau-Ponty, 1964/1968, p. 123). Through this embrace, Merleau-Ponty (1964/1968) argued, embodied intersubjectivity opens on to, and discloses the Other. "Others and my body are born together from the original ecstasy" (Merleau-Ponty, 1960/1964b, p. 174).

Merleau-Ponty's (1964/1968) metaphor of the intertwining opens up the possibility of empathy being understood as a process where the Other and the observer become one. For other phenomenological philosophers, however, the dissolution of the boundaries between the Other and the observer is potentially problematic. Stein (1916/1989), for example, argued that it is vital that a dissolution of boundaries does not take place. If it did, *Einfülung* would no longer entail understanding the Other's experience from their perspective. Instead, the focus would have shifted back to the researcher's subjectivity. "Empathy is not a feeling of oneness" (1916/1989, p. 17), Stein asserted. Understanding comes from perceiving the differences between the Other and the observer. The selfness of "I," she argued, is "brought into relief in contrast with the otherness of the other" (1916/1989, p. 38).

Husserl's (1952/1989) notion that one's experience of the world is intersubjective, full of people who are similar to and different from oneself perhaps offers a compromise. In the intersubjective space people move within and between; they see similarities and differences; sometimes they see themselves in others and, at other times, they see others in themselves. Sometimes individuals touch, at other times they are touched. The "intertwining" encompasses this movement.

Applied to the research process, one can see this in practice where one dances between different subjective and intersubjective moments. Through a process of hermeneutic reflection, people can begin to capture the way the Other, the self, and the intersubjective space move in and out of focus (Finlay, 2003a). Through this phenomenological reflection, one can begin to disentangle how others present themselves to and through oneself.

DISCUSSION

Interpermeating Layers and Hermeneutic Reflection

I have offered a layered understanding of reflexive embodied empathy as a movement from subjectively feeling into the meanings of another's embodiment through to an awareness of more thorough going embodied intersubjectivity. The first layer, connecting of, suggests one way of tuning into another's bodily way of being through using one's own embodied reactions. The second layer, acting into, calls attention to the way existences (beings) are intertwined in a dynamic of doubling and mirroring. The third layer, merging with, involves a "reciprocal insertion and intertwining" (Merleau-Ponty, 1964/1968, p. 138) of others in the individual and of the individual in them. Through the web that is intersubjectivity, one comes to understand that self-understanding and other-understanding are intimately interwoven.

Taken as a whole, there is a subtle shift from an awareness of the Other's body as linked to mine to an appreciation of the "we," where world and body are understood to be intertwined with one another. "Once a body-world relationship is recognized, there is a ramification of my body and a ramification of the world and a correspondence between its inside and my outside and my inside and its outside" (Merelau-Ponty, 1964/1968, p. 136).

However, having suggested three layers as somewhat separate levels of empathy, I need also to reemphasize their interpermeation and coexistence. People fluidly move in, out, and through different depths (or intensities) of empathy during each moment of any relational engagement. They are not sequential; instead, they coexist as possibilities of experience. As McCleary (1960/1964) put it, "My body teaches me to know the simultaneous presence of multiple perspectives" (p. xvii). In one moment researchers might find themselves observing the participant and discover some linking experience that enables the researchers' empathy. In the next moment, they could be sucked down into the deep, experiencing an intense intertwining with the participant. Different dimensions of experience and being are called to the fore. Researchers also simultaneously inhabit different layers. For instance, in my mirroring of Kath's embodied experience (layer 2), I was aware of what my own embodied responses would be in her place (layer 1). At the same time, I felt that I was her (layer 3). Here, a moment of *acting into* is also lived as *connecting of* and *merging with*. The layers of empathy are thus not mutually exclusive, and are perhaps better characterized dynamically as fluid moments of empathic experience.

The challenge for the researcher is to reflexively exploit the opportunities offered by these different layers through an iterative and dialectical process of hermeneutic reflection (Finlay, 2003a). Part of this reflective process involves a dancing in and out of the relational involvement. Todres (1990) made a similar point in reference to psychotherapy, describing how a therapist might develop a rhythm of interactive being with, where closeness and distance are simultaneously maintained. The challenge, as Todres saw it, lies in:

> being close enough to the immediacy of the situation to experience what is happening, yet also to be able to distance oneself from such immediacy in order to become interested in the quality of interaction as a phenomenon. It is this latter ability that gives the therapist a much needed degree of freedom; a freedom that allows him or her to focus on the quality of the interaction with some degree of empathy. (1990, p. 40)

In another extract from my reflexive diary, written as I was immersed in some phenomenological analysis, I show how that sense of closeness and distance combine. In the extract, I simultaneously inhabit intertwined roles of researcher, participant, therapist, and client.

> It's like seeing simultaneous reflections in multiple mirrors. As I dwell with the transcripts of conversations between participants and myself, the images become blurred and identities converge. The therapist I am interviewing becomes my client. The "I" who is both researcher and therapist divides and I slide inadvertently into my therapist body. As therapist, I feel a familiar sensation in my belly—a stirring of excitement as emotional empathy expands. I experience a sense of "humble-power." I feel honored as the participant opens herself, discloses secrets, shares her tears. I know something of the power I have used to "facilitate" this. Yet, simultaneously, I feel powerless and helpless. What can I do in the face of this distress? I am not her therapist. Then, as I witness her strength, wisdom, caring, I am reminded that she is a therapist herself with a capacity and her own ways to cope. Then images converge again and a new relationship comes into focus. Suddenly, I am the client, feeling tears, needing solace, wanting this caring, listening therapist to nurture and reassure me. Then a point of interest captures my professional attention. The axis spins, and I find myself being the researcher. I can stand back now and draw a cloak of power around

me once more as I select what to hear, what to report. I decide how to represent my participants and which stories I tell. (Finlay, 2003a, pp. 111–113)

This example demonstrates how complex layers of intersubjective understanding emerge out of moments of empathy. Engaged in understanding my participant, I am also engaged in self-understanding.

Implications for Research Method:
Collaboration and Reflexivity

All three layers of empathy operate from and through intersubjectivity. Put another way, echoing Husserl (1952/1989), the relational space between participant and researcher is the site of disclosure of the Other and of any understanding which comes about. This point needs to be taken seriously when researchers choose a methodology. What methods will allow a glimpse into the relationship between participant–researcher? How can one begin to capture intersubjective meanings? The limitations of simply analyzing written research protocols or just focusing on participants' words in transcripts are clear. Instead, scientists need methods with a greater focus on the dialogue between researcher and researched. They also need to encourage a reflexivity in researchers and participants to attend, as much as possible, to their mutual embodied experiencing (Burns, 2003).

Walsh (2004) picked up these points in his discussion of embodied reflexivity. Drawing on Gadamer's distinction between statements and speculative language, Walsh argued that qualitative research must not lose sight of the discursive foundation on which reflexivity lies. Such research must explore the ways in which language is itself embodied. It should be conscious of how researchers can all too easily disembody their participants through certain positions or procedures. He recommended replacing traditional "nondirective" interviews (where the researcher can—paradoxically—be perceived as critical and judgmental) with "dialogues" where the participant is an engaged, embodied coparticipant. He went on to recommend explicit researcher reflexivity:

The researcher "slackens the intentional threads which attach us to the world and this brings them to our notice" (Merleau-Ponty, 1945, cited in Aanstoos, 1983, p. 253). I suggest that the phrase, "slackening intentional threads" is a way of characterizing embodied reflexivity, in that it points to both allowing for the play of conversation and to examining the context in which the conversation unfolds. For interpretive analysis this means that the conversation rather than a participant's "protocol" is the object of analysis, and that the structure interpreted is intersubjective. Hence the researcher's indelible presence within the conversation must be made explicit and remain explicit throughout all levels of analysis. (Walsh, 2004, p. 116–117)

Burns (in press) made a similar point in her discussion of interviewing as embodied communication. Here, meanings are seen as the product of reciprocal dynamic "physical" exchanges between researcher and participant. "Embodied reflexivity," Burns said, "can be deployed to interrogate ethical commitments, guide research discussions, enrich analyses, provide an adjunct corpus of reflexivity data, and contribute to the development of theories of embodied subjectivity."

A number of other collaborative approaches have been developed, which focus on the conversation or apply reflexivity explicitly. For instance, in a variant of reflexivity known as *mutual collaboration* (Finlay, 2003b), participants may be enlisted as co-researchers. Also, researchers may themselves become participants as they engage in cycles of mutual reflection and experience. Adopting this latter method, Ellis, Kiesinger, and Tillmann-Healy (1997, p. 121) offered some fascinating insights into how an empathic research relationship can develop, and in turn shape the findings of the research. In this study, the researchers explored their personal experiences of bulimia and their empathy for the Other:

> Lisa and I are masters at intellectualizing bulimia. Through our conversations, I have moved beyond a literal interpretation of bulimia as being only about thinness to thinking about how eating disorders also speak to personal longings. But, it always has been hard for us to focus on emotional issues. I have come to see this as a *relational* [emphasis added] problem to which we both contribute. ... Bulimia is about mess. Lisa and I talk about it, study it, analyze it, and We Do IT! As perfectionists ... we craft exteriors that contradict the mess in our lives. Still I know what goes on "behind closed doors" in Lisa's life, because I know what goes on behind my own closed doors" (Ellis et al., 1997, pp. 127–8).

Mutuality and Self-Understanding

If one understands empathy as arising through an intersubjective relationship, one also needs to recognize that a mutual dialectic takes place. In research terms, researchers are reminded to attend reflexively to their impact on the participants and the participants on them. Always, researchers affect and are affected by their participants in a process of *reciprocal transformation*. As we have a capacity to empathize with the Other, they can empathize with us.

In the "reciprocal insertion and intertwining," as Merleau-Ponty has shown, researchers are called to the Other in a double-belongingness. Empathy is not a one-way process. It is not just the researcher imagining himself in the participant's place. It is understanding the participant as an Other who, in turn, sees the researcher as an Other in himself. It involves the possibility of seeing oneself from the Other's perspective. "I live in the facial expressions of the other, as I feel him living in mine" (Merleau-Ponty, 1960/1964b, p. 146). Here, mutual intersubjective engagement transcends any first-person singular perspective as it shifts the center of orientation. Normally, people experience the world in terms of egocentric space. They experience themselves as being "here" with things around them. When they experience another, the Other is "there" in relation to the person's "here." However, as Husserl (1952/1989) recognized, with empathy the orientation shifts as one begins to see the Other's "here" and appreciates one's orientation is just one among others (Thompson, 2001).

Then, having empathetically grasped the Other's perception, one's own sense of self-identity is nudged, even challenged. "We are literally what others think of us," asserted Merleau-Ponty (1945/1962, p. 106). Stein (1916/1989) elaborated this idea in her discussion of what she called "reiterated empathy." To paraphrase her argument, seeing the Other's empathic experience, one sees oneself from the Other's perspective of one and one gains another view of oneself. This, in turn, shapes one's self-identity. Husserl made a similar point: "When I realize that I can be an *alter ego* for the other just as he can be it for me, a marked change in my own constitutive significance takes place" (Husserl, 1973, paraphrased by Zahavi, 2001, p. 160). Thompson, too, described this process: "I experience myself as recognizably sentient 'from without,' that is, from your perspective, the perspective of another. In this way, one's sense of self-identity, even at the most fundamental level of embodied agency, is inseparable from recognition by another" (Thompson, 2001, pp. 19–20).

Stein (1916/1989) took the idea further:

> At the end of the empathic process ... there is a new objectification ... now ... it has a new dignity because what was presented as empty has found its fulfillment ... "I" can become conscious of itself, even though it is not necessarily "awake." (1989, p. 60)

When applied to the research process, this mutuality raises a number of questions. When researchers empathize with their participant, just who and what is being revealed? When I merged with Jenny, was it Jenny I saw or was it myself? Perhaps, in the end, intersubjectivity demands that empathic revelation of an Other and reflexive uncovering of self are inseparable. "Since the seer is caught up in what he sees, it is still himself he sees. There is a fundamental narcissism of all vision" (Merleau-Ponty, 1964/1968, p. 139).

CONCLUSION

In this article, I have explored the theory and philosophy of empathy from a phenomenological perspective and applied these ideas to the research process. Empathy can be understood as feeling with the Other—a reciprocal process where one seeks to find ways to allow the Other to present him- or herself to and through one. It involves an intersubjective process of imaginal self-transposition and mutual identification where self-understanding and Other-understanding is inter-twined. Through different examples of reflexive analysis from my research, I have tried to show how our intersubjective corporeal commonality enables the possibility of empathy and how, in turn, it is that empathy which enables understanding of the Other and self-understanding.

Applying these ideas to research, I emphasize the importance of attending to the relationship with participants. More specifically, researchers' experience of the embodied intersubjective relationship needs to be probed as part of the process of hermeneutic reflection. Explicitly and consciously engaging in the practice of reflexive embodied empathy in terms of connecting of, acting into, and merging-with offers a way of capturing something of the interpermeation of body and world.

ACKNOWLEDGMENTS

My grateful thanks go to Scott Churchill for reminding me to return to Husserl's work on intersubjectivity to better anchor my concept of reflexive embodied empathy. I am also indebted to Maree Burns, who first drew my attention to the idea of embodied reflexivity.

REFERENCES

Aanstoos, C. (1983). The think aloud method in descriptive research. *Journal of Phenomenological Psychology, 13,* 243–266.

Aanstoos, C. M. (1991). Embodiment as ecstatic intertwining. In C. M. Aanstoos (Ed.). *Studies in humanistic psychology* (pp. 94–111). Carrollton, GA: West Georgia College.

Burns, M. (2003). Interviewing: Embodied communication. *Feminism & Psychology, 13,* 229–236.

Burns, M. (in press). Bodies that speak: Examining the dialogues in research interactions. *Qualitative Research in Psychology.*

Churchill, S. D. (2000–2001). Intercorporeality, gestural communication, and the voices of silence: Towards a phenomenological ethology (Part 1). *Somatics, 13,* 28–32.

Churchill, S. (2003). Gestural communication with a Bonobo: Empathy, alerity, and carnal intersubjectivity. *Constructivism and the Human Sciences, 8*(1), 19–36.

Churchill, S. D., Lowery, J. E., McNally, O., & Rao, A. (1998). The question of reliability in interpretive psychological research: A comparison of three phenomenologically based protocol analyses. In R. Valle (Ed.), *Phenomenological inquiry in psychology: Existential and transpersonal dimensions* (pp. 63–85). New York: Plenum Press.

Davidson, L. (2003). *Living outside mental illness: Qualitative studies of recovery in schizophrenia.* New York: New York University Press.

Davis, M. H.(1994). *Empathy: A social psychological approach.* Oxford, UK: Westview Press.

Depraz, N. (2001). The Husserlian theory of intersubjectivity as alterology. In E. Thompson (Ed.), *Between ourselves: Second-person issues in the study of consciousness* (pp. 169–178). Thorverton, UK: Imprint Academic.

Dilthey, W. (1977). The understanding of other persons and their expression of life (K. L. Heiges, Trans.). In W. Dilthey, *Descriptive psychology and historical understanding* (pp. 123–144). The Hague: Martinus Nijhoff. (Original work published 1927)

Ellis, C., Kiesinger, C. E., & Tillmann-Healy, L. M. (1997). Interactive interviewing: Talking about emotional experience. In R. Hertz (Ed.), *Reflexivity and voice* (pp. 119–149). Thousand Oaks, CA: Sage.

Finlay, L. (2003a). Through the looking glass: Intersubjectivity and hermeneutic reflection. In L. Finlay and B. Gough (Eds.), *Reflexivity: A practical guide for researchers in health and social sciences* (pp. 105–119). Oxford: Blackwell Science.

Finlay, L. (2003b). The reflexive journey: Mapping multiple routes. In L. Finlay & B. Gough (Eds.), *Reflexivity: A practical guide for researchers in health and social sciences* (pp. 3–20). Oxford: Blackwell Science.

Finlay, L., Smith, J. A., King, N., Langdridge, D., Butt, T., & Ashworth, P. (forthcoming). "What Can I Trust?": A polyvocal, phenomenological analysis of the psychology of mistrust. *Qualitative Research in Psychology.*

Gadamer, H.-G. (1989). *Truth and method* (2nd rev. ed.). London: Sheed & Ward.

Gallico, P. (1970). *Jennie.* London: Penguin Books.

Gendlin, E.T. (1981). *Focusing* (2nd ed. New rev. instructions). New York: Bantam Books.

Halling, S., & Goldfarb, M. (1991). Grounding truth in the body: Therapy and research renewed. *The Humanistic Psychologist, 19,* 313–330.

Husserl, E. (1959). *Erste philosophie II (1923–1924).* Husserliana VIII [First philosophy. Second part: Theory of phenomenological reduction]. Den Haag: M. J. Nijhoff.

Husserl, E. (1966). *Analysen zur passiven Synthesis, Hua XI* [Analyses concerning passive and active synthesis]. Den Haag: M. J. Nijoff.

Husserl, E. (1970). *The crisis of European sciences and transcendental phenomenology* (D. Carr, Trans.). Evanston, Ill.: Northwestern University Press. (Original work published 1936).

Husserl, E. (1973). *Zur phanomenologie der intersubjektivitat I,* [On the phenomenology of intersubjectivity, part one], Husserliana XIII. Den Haag: M. Nijhoff.

Husserl, E. (1974). *Formule Und transzendentale logick,* [Formal and trancendental logic], Husserliana XVLII. Den Haag: M. Nijhoff.

Husserl, E. (1989). *Ideas pertaining to a pure phenomenology and to a phenomenological philosophy, second book: Studies in the phenomenology of constitution* (R. Rojcewicz & A. Schuwer, Trans.). Boston: Kluwer. (Original work written in 1928 and published posthumously in 1952)

Levin, D. M. (1988). Transpersonal phenomenology: The corporeal schema. *The Humanistic Psychologist, 16,* 282–313.

McCleary, R. C. (1964). Translator's introduction. In M. Merleau-Ponty (Ed.), *Signs* (R. C. McCleary, Trans., pp. ix–xxxii). Evanston, Il: Northwestern University Press. (Original work published 1960).

Merleau-Ponty, M. (1962). *Phenomenology of perception* (C. Smith, Trans.). London: Routledge & Kegan Paul. (Original work published 1945).

Merleau-Ponty, M. (1964a). Eye and mind. In J. Edie (Ed.), *The primacy of perception* (pp. 159–190). Evanston, IL: Northwestern University Press. (Original work published 1961)

Merleau-Ponty, M. (1964b). *Signs* (R. C. McCleary, Trans.). Evanston, Il: Northwestern University Press. (Original work published 1960)

Merleau-Ponty, M. (1968). *The visible and the invisible* (A. Lingis, Trans.). Evanston, IL: Northwestern University Press. (Original work published 1964).

O'Hara, M. (1997). Relational empathy: Beyond modernist egocentricism to postmodern holistic contextualism. In A. C. Bohart & L. S. Greenberg (Eds.), *Empathy reconsidered* (pp. 295–319). Washington, DC: American Psychological Association.

Peloquin, S. M. (1995). The fullness of empathy: Reflections and illustrations. *The American Journal of Occupational Therapy, 49,* 24–31.

Rogers, C. R. (1975). Empathic: An unappreciated way of being. *Counseling Psychologist, 5,* 2–10.

Spiegelberg, H. (1975). *Doing phenomenology: Essays on and in phenomenology.* The Hague, The Netherlands: Martinus Nijhoff.

Stein, E. (1989). *On the problem of empathy* (3rd ed.; W. Stein, trans.). Washington, D.C.: ICS Publications. (Original work published 1916).

Thompson, E. (2001). Empathy and consciousness. In E. Thompson (Ed.), *Between ourselves: second-person issues in the study of consciousness* (pp. 1–32). Thorverton, UK: Imprint Academic.

Thompson, E. (2005). *Empathy and human experience.* In J. D. Proctor (Ed.), *Science, religion, and the human experience* (pp. 260–285). Oxford, UK: Oxford University Press.

Todres, L. A. (1990). The rhythm of psychotherapeutic attention: A training model. *Journal of Phenomenological Psychology, 21,* 32–45.

Walsh, R. (2004). The methodological implications of Gadamer's distinction between statements and speculative language. *The Humanistic Psychologist, 32,* 105–119.

Zahavi, D. (2001). Beyond empathy: Phenomenological approaches to intersubjectivity. In E. Thompson (Ed.), *Between ourselves: Second-person issues in the study of consciousness* (pp. 151–167). Thorverton, UK: Imprint Academic.

AUTHOR NOTE

Linda Finlay, PhD is a freelance Academic Consultant. She teaches and writes with the Open University (Milton Keynes, UK) and she supervises postgraduate dissertations at the University of East London (UK). She qualified in 1977 as an occupational therapist and then became an academic psychologist after obtaining her psychology honors degree and PhD with the Open University. She is best known for her textbooks on occupational therapy, her work on reflexivity in qualitative research and her phenomenological research on the experience of multiple sclerosis. Since 2003, she has published three books: *The Practice of Psychosocial Occupational Therapy* (Nelson Thornes); *Qualitative Research for Health Professionals: Challenging Choices* (Whurr Publications), a volume coedited with Claire Ballinger; and *Reflexivity: A Practical Guide for Researchers in Health and Social Science* (Blackwell Publishing), a volume coedited with Brendan Gough. Her current research interests include the lived experience of trauma.

THE HUMANISTIC PSYCHOLOGIST, 33(4), 293–303

Finding and Correcting Flawed Research Literatures

Edward A. Delgado-Romero

Department of Educational Psychology
University of Georgia

George S. Howard

Department of Psychology
University of Notre Dame

Humanistic psychology has always viewed scientific psychology with skepticism. Good reasons for this skepticism continuously appear. One is then left with the choice, "Is a scientific approach to humans inherently wrongheaded?" or "Is scientific psychology an imperfect but improving enterprise?" This article reviews another domain where research in scientific psychology proves misleading.

Suppose a psychologist was asked a question such as, "Is psychotherapy effective?" or "Is remote intercessory prayer effective?" or "Do humans possess psychic powers?" How might a psychologist reply? The most common strategy would be to conduct a meta-analysis over the relevant research literature and report the results. In all 3 cases (i.e., psychotherapy, efficacy of remote intercessory prayer, and telepathic powers) the answer would be a significant, positive effect size, suggesting that all 3 are real, efficacious phenomena. Unfortunately, in at least 2 of the 3 cases, the literature likely gives an incorrect answer to the question. How can one show that some literatures yield "incorrect" answers to research queries, whereas other literatures give "correct" answers? Finally, how should psychology's publication practices change to avoid flawed literatures?

For well over a century, a strain of thought in psychology has been skeptical of the scientific analysis of persons (Bakan, 1967; James, 1950). Around the middle of the last century, many of the voices of protest coalesced in the humanistic

Correspondence should be addressed to George Howard, Department of Psychology, University of Notre Dame, 218 Haggar Hall, Notre Dame, IN   46556. E-mail: Howard.2@nd.edu

psychology movement (Giorgi, 1970; Mair, 1989; Rogers, 1973; Wertz, 1992). A central tenet of humanistic psychology has been skepticism of a natural science approach to psychology, and the desire for a "human science" alternative (Giorgi, 1970, 1992). Although the development of a human science alternative has made some progress, humanistic psychology's larger impact has come as a critique of the natural science excesses of mainstream psychological research (Giorgi, 1970; Howard, 1982; Howard & Conway, 1986; Rogers, 1973). This article reviews yet another glaring problem with natural science research with humans and the need for (at least) a revision of psychology's current research practices.

In earlier programs of research, my colleagues and I found flaws in mainstream research methodologies regarding the value of retrospective pretests (e.g., Howard, Ralph, et al, 1979), use of behavior versus self-report measures (e.g., Howard, Maxwell, Wiener, Boynton, & Rooney, 1980), and the proportion of variance in human behavior due to free will (e.g., Howard & Conway, 1986). In each research program a "softer" or more humanistic alternative methodology was actually found that was more valid than a "harder" or more behavioral methodology that was favored in natural science, psychological research. The philosophy of science behind this empirical upgrading of accepted methodologies is laid out in Howard (1982).

A recent program of research (Howard, Hill, et al, 2005; Howard, Lau, et al, 2005; Lau, Howard, Maxwell, & Venter, 2005; Sweeny & Howard, 2005) suggested that there are problems with several research literatures in psychology. These problems are caused by the discipline's preference for significant, rather than nonsignificant, findings in deciding which articles will be published and which will not. This preference is often overtly stated, for example in the APA publication manual (2001) and in the editorial statements made by journal editors. It does not matter whether the decision to publish "good" (statistically significant results) or not to pursue or publish "bad" (nonsignificant findings) is made by a journal editor, a reviewer, or researchers themselves. It is problematic because any preference for "good" over "bad" findings leads to a biased—and sometimes severely misleading—research literature.

Imagine a baseball player who computes his batting average by only including days on which he got one or more hits (his good days) and eliminates days when he did not get any hits (his bad days). Obviously, his computed batting average (e.g., .600) would represent a gross distortion of his "real" (i.e., when all at bats are included) batting average (e.g., .300). This represents an analogy to the classic file drawer (Rosenthal, 1979) problem in psychological research. If one "reclaims" one half of the player's days from the file drawer, one could correct the misleading literature (e.g., .600) somewhat (e.g., batting average goes from .600 to .450). Although this corrected average is a more accurate estimate than the original batting average, it is still wrong (i.e., the "Truth" is .300, not .450).[1] Although all attempts to correct flawed meta-analyses yield improved estimates, unless one identifies all the studies in the "file drawer" (which is a virtual impossibility) the resulting estimate is "better," but still incorrect.

A METHOD FOR FINDING FLAWED LITERATURES— A NEW MOUSETRAP

Suppose one wanted to determine the extent to which the literature suggesting the effectiveness of psychotherapy is biased by the file drawer effect. The literature (Lambert & Bergin, 1994) suggests that the average treatment subject would be at the 80th percentile (instead of the 50th percentile) of a comparable control group at posttest. One way to test the validity of the psychotherapy effectiveness literature is to begin forming a new literature where there is no possibility of a file drawer effect. To do so, one must conduct several studies and accept all results (regardless of whether or not they reached statistical significance) that are obtained by methodologically adequate studies.

Imagine there are two different possibilities: the present literature is exactly correct (i.e., the average treatment subject percentile across new studies is .80, as Smith, Glass, and Miller, 1980 reported) or; the present literature is based solely on Type I errors (i.e., the average treatment percentile is .50, which would occur when the treatment and control groups means are identical). That is, imagine 100 studies were conducted and only 4 of them obtained significant findings. Further, the truth (if all 100 studies were published) is that treatment is not effective. However, if the literature consisted of only the four significant effects, which were the only studies published, then the literature would be based only on the four published Type I errors.

Now imagine that one conducted four studies (with a sample size of each study close to the average for the literature in question) and the treatment subjects' percentiles were .74, 62, .89, and .77. The average percentile of .76 looks very close to the literature's value of .80. Thus, one would tentatively conclude that the literature appears to be contaminated very little (or not at all) by the file drawer effect. This is because, if the null were true (i.e., 50th percentile), it is extremely unlikely that four independent studies would achieve results of .74, .62, .89, and .79. Still, our

---

[1]Meta-analysts have developed a number of adjustment methods in an effort to eliminate the effect of publication bias on estimating the true effect size (e.g., Duvall & Tweedie, 2000; Hedges & Vevea, 1996; Iyengar & Greenhouse, 1988). Although such methods can be helpful in reducing the effects of publication bias, current research suggests that even the most sophisticated of the methods developed so far cannot uniformly be relied on to eliminate bias (Kraemer, Gardner, Brooks, & Yesavage, 1998; Macaskill, Wallter, & Irwig, 2001).

conclusion must be tentative, because all the new studies would have been conducted by one research team. Thus, one would want to invite other researchers to replicate the findings in their labs, to insure that the data are representative.

Conversely, imagine the average percentile among treatment subjects in the four studies was .48 (e.g., .50, .46, .51, .45). Here one would tentatively conclude that the literature appears to be badly flawed, as these data are extremely unlikely if the real value was .80 (as the literature suggests). Again, further generalization replications would be required. Finally, one needs to conduct as many studies as are necessary to reasonably favor one outcome (i.e., .80, suggesting the existing literature is adequate) over the other (i.e., .50, the literature appears to be misleading).

BUT WILL IT CATCH MICE?

In an effort to test the proposed methodology for identifying flawed research literatures, we first considered the domain of implementation intentions (i.e., where people are forced to concretize, by writing them, their behavioral intentions; Gollwitzer, 1999). This literature was selected because we (Howard, Hill, et al., 2005) disagreed among ourselves as to the construct's likely efficacy (as opposed to the psychotherapy outcome literature, where we all thought that psychotherapy would be efficacious). The research literature on implementation intentions suggested an average effect size of $d = .54$ (a medium effect size, cf. Cohen, 1969) which was contrasted with a d of .00, which would imply the literature is solely the result of Type I errors.

Three studies testing the efficacy of implementation intentions relative to proper control groups found an average d score of .49. This finding was so close to our meta-analysis of the research literature ($d = .54$) that it seems the existent literature is relatively free of debilitating file drawer effects (as $d = .00$ is very unlikely). Although it was reassuring to find that a literature stood up well to our scrutiny, we desired to see if the methodology could identify a literature that would not stand up to scrutiny (i.e., a flawed literature).

The next construct that the team members disagreed on was the emerging literature that suggests the causal efficacy of remote intercessory prayer (Harris et al., 1999). The meta-analysis revealed a small but significant effect size of $d = .21$. Our three new studies averaged an effect size of $d = .02$, suggesting that the existing literature might be based on Type I errors, because $d = .02$ is clearly closer to $d = .00$ than it is to $d = .21$. Of course, replications of our findings by other researchers would be required before stating a definitive conclusion. However, our technique seems to be able to pick up problematic research literatures. Thus, it seems likely that the many psychologists who tout the proven efficacy of remote intercessory prayer are basing their claims on a flawed, misleading literature.

The remaining constructs to be tested were selected because we suspected the existing literatures might be misleading. The *Mozart effect* suggests that participants score higher on certain IQ subscales immediately after listening to a Mozart sonata rather than when participants are exposed to a variety of attention placebos. The most recent meta-analysis (Hetland, 2000) suggested an average effect size of $d = .46$ for the Mozart effect. Three studies were conducted and yielded an average effect size of $d = -.14$ (Sweeny, 2005). Again a $d = -.14$ is much closer to $d = .00$ than it is to the literature's value of $d = .46$. Thus, our data suggest that the existing literature on the Mozart effect is also problematic. Again, further generalization studies are required before stating strong conclusions.

To this point, only three studies have been required to render tentative decisions on the adequacy of various research literatures. Our last research literature (Howard, Lau, et al., 2005; Lau et al., 2005) required considerably more than three studies to untangle. The question was, "Do humans possess telepathic powers?" Although most psychologists believe humans are not psychic, the research literature argues strongly that humans are psychic (see Bem & Honorton, 1994, and Storm & Ertel, 2001, for positive meta-analyses). However, even after more than 80 years of research, the issue remains unresolved (see Milton & Wiseman, 1999, for a negative meta-analysis). First, we need to explain a bit of why the research picture is currently so unclear.

The strongest methodological procedure for testing humans' telepathic power is the ganzfeld procedure, although the literature includes many other approaches for testing humans' psychic powers. In the ganzfeld procedure, participants try to choose a target picture out of an array of four pictures as the dependant variable. Thus, participants must beat a precise chance level (25%) of correct choices to demonstrate psychic ability. For clarity's sake, all results will be expressed as percentage correct scores rather than d scores. The two positive meta-analyses found percent correct responses of .32 (Bem & Honorton, 1994) and .31 (Storm & Ertel, 2001). These findings suggest that a few people (but a statistically significant number) possess telepathic powers. But, because these psychics are mixed in with the 25% who are not psychic, but who correctly identify the target picture by chance, identification of the true psychics (if such people exist) is not possible.

The negative meta-analysis (Milton & Wiseman, 1999) found a hit rate of 27% where results from only the methodologically stronger ganzfeld procedure were included.[2] One should note that the results of the negative meta-analysis and the positive meta-analyses were quite close to one another (from 27% to 32%).

---

[2]Milton and Wiseman (1999) employed a rather puzzling form of meta-analysis. They reviewed 30 studies and weighted each study equally (i.e., unweighted procedure), rather than the widely accepted procedure of weighting each study by the study's sample size (i.e., weighted procedure). Thus, one study that ran only 4 pairs of subjects received the same weighting in the overall Effect Size (ES) as did another that tested 100 pairs. Using the more common weighted procedure, the mean ES more than doubled from .013 to .028.

In our first study (Lau et al., 2005), we found that a significant (45%) group of participants chose the correct target. In the second study, 40% chose the correct picture, and 20% correct choices were made in our third study. Although the percent correct hits across the three studies (i.e., 35%) was greater than even the positive meta-analyses, this overall percentage was not significantly greater than chance. These conflicting results led us to conduct five more studies, obtaining correct percentages of 30%, 30%, 20%, 35%, and 40%. After eight studies, we had an overall hit rate of 32% (which agrees with the positive meta-analyses) and, in fact, our hit rate was also statistically significant, $\chi^2(1) = 4.03$, $p < .05$. Further, when our data are added to the Milton and Wiseman (1999) meta-analysis over ganzfeld studies, the overall percent correct responses goes from 26% to 27% and this value now is very close to significant. So, for the moment, even the evidence against humans possessing psychic powers is precariously close to demonstrating humans do have psychic powers. The lower boundary of the confidence interval is now 24.7%, which is extremely close to not including the 25% value.

AFTER FURTHER REVIEW ...

In the National Football League, the referees call every play and their decision on the field stands—unless it is challenged by one of the team's coaches. The head referee then looks at the challenged play on videotape (which provides a very different perspective on the play), and the referee uses the videotape to determine if there is sufficient evidence on the videotape to warrant overturning the call made on the field. Because no humans are perfect, it is wise to periodically overturn decisions, if the evidence from a somewhat different perspective warrants the change. Referees announce their decision, to either uphold their call on the field or to reverse themselves, with the phrase, "After further review... ."

To this point, our research team's data suggested that the literatures on remote intercessory prayer and the Mozart effect were problematic. We are comfortable with those conclusions, and hope generalization studies will begin immediately. Our data also suggested that the implementation intentions literature is solid, and we see no reason to further test that construct. Finally, although our own data (and the data of many others) suggest that some humans possess psychic powers, the team is still very uncomfortable with that conclusion. Thus, we initiated a further review of the ganzfeld procedure and the data obtained when using it.

In the ganzfeld procedure, participants are run in pairs. According to psychic theory, if one member of the pair is psychic (P) but the other is not (n) there will be no transmission of information. Only PP pairs can successfully send and receive messages. What exactly does this imply?

If one were to obtain only a chance level of correct responses, one would have five chance hits in every 20-pair study. What number of correct hits would be expected if every participant was a P? Here, all pairings would be PP, so the expected number of correct choices would be 20 (assuming PP pairs always correctly send and receive messages).

Now consider an intermediate situation. Imagine one in four people are psychic, which is an interesting possibility, and that Ps always successfully send and receive messages. What would be the expected value for a 20-pair study? It would be less than 20, but more than 5, obviously. Exactly what would one think the expected value would be?

It turns out the expected value is a paltry 5.95, and all the data in the telepathy research obtains values of this magnitude. Why does the expected value fall so precipitously from 20 (when all are Ps) to only 5.95 (when 25% are Ps)? The probability of the sender being psychic is 1/4 and the probability of the receiver being a P is also 1/4. It follows that there is only 1 PP pair in every 16 pairs! Thus, in a 20-pair study, one would expect (on average) five correct chance hits plus 1.25 PP hits, minus the likelihood that the chance hits might involve a PP pair (or .30). Why is this dramatic drop in the expected value for the ganzfeld procedure so important? It is because it makes a very small deviation from chance (5.95 – 5. = .95) all that one can reasonably hope to obtain, when an interesting phenomenon (25% of participants are psychic) is posited. The interpretation of studies with low statistical power is problematic. We now have unearthed a methodological parallel—the ganzfeld procedure is (methodologically) far less powerful than any of us had imagined. Finally, this reduced methodological power is caused by too low a ratio (1/4) of Ps to total participants. Is there any way of enriching this ratio?

Shortly after our sixth telepathy study, we hit upon a method for increasing the proportion of Ps in our sample. Suppose we considered only the pairs that chose the correct picture in our last two studies as participants in a different kind of study. What would be the ratio of P to total participants in that group? If the Ps were 25% in the original group, there would be 43% Ps in the group that answered correctly. This means that more than one in four pairs are PP in this enhanced sample. This represents a four-fold improvement on the 1/16 likelihood of PP pairs in the original studies.

We also realized that our confidence in our findings would be greatly enhanced if pairs went through the ganzfeld procedure four times, instead of just once. We paid pairs $100 if they would participate in the second part of our study. Out of the final 40 pairs, 15 pairs chose the correct picture. Of these 15 pairs, 13 pairs agreed to participate in a second (four-trial) study.

Because each pair had a one-in-four correct by chance probability in the four-trial study, exactly one correct response was expected by chance. Pairs that got zero or one (chance level) pictures correct would (likely) not be PP pairs. Pairs that got two correct might be a PP pair, but also might be a pair that was slightly luckier than chance. Any pairs getting three or four correct pictures (out of four) would likely be PP pairs. If the null was true, the number of pairs who got two or more correct answers should have equaled the number of pairs who got zero correct (because one correct choice is the chance level).

Of our 13 pairs, there were no fours or threes; 1 pair got two correct; 5 pairs had one correct picture; and 7 pairs had no correct responses. These are enormously disappointing data for individuals who believe humans possess psychic powers—especially because the sample had undergone a selection procedure to increase the percentage of Ps in the sample. Due to this last data set, we do not believe that humans possess telepathic powers. Further, the approximately 32% correct figure obtained in an enormous number of psi studies remains perplexing. Perhaps this 7% phenomenon is comparable to Meehl's (1978) "crud factor," which suggests that everything is correlated with everything else to a small degree. Meehl cited this as evidence that a null hypothesis is never literally true. Or, perhaps it simply reflects our enduring preference for significant results over studies that obtain nonsignificant findings.

CONCLUSIONS

Sometimes it is necessary for a science to first take a step backward, then take two steps forward. Psychology's research literatures now seem to be more problematic than most had imagined. This difficulty is caused by the discipline's preference for significant findings over nonsignificant effects when deciding which studies will be published and which will be discarded. This situation is clearly a step backward for the discipline.

The procedure described herein represents a promising technique for sorting adequate research literatures (i.e., implementation intentions) from the more problematic research literatures (i.e., remote intercessory prayer, the Mozart effect). And in some instances (i.e., psychic powers) the answers still are a bit unclear. This new methodology appears to be a promising method for sorting the grain from the chaff. Are there any ways to construct research literatures that will not be problematic?

There are two very different solutions to this problem. The first solution has the benefit of allowing us to keep our classical null hypothesis testing statistics. Researchers would submit only the introduction and methods sections of their articles. Reviews of these sections determine whether the results (whatever they might be) will be published. This procedure would give an equal likelihood of being published to good (significant) and bad (nonsignificant) results.

The second solution is actually better, but it requires greater disruption of psychology's publishing process. We recommend that Bayesian statistics replace the current classical (Fischerian or frequentist) statistical techniques. Any scientist is most interested in the question "What is the likelihood that my theory (e.g., that humans have psychic powers, that remote intercessory prayer produces real effects, etc.) is true, given my data?" That would be the probability of my theory given the data (T/D). Is that what our statistical techniques now compute? Absolutely not! They calculate the probability of D/not T (this data set given the null).

Given that our statistical techniques calculate something other than what scientists desire (T/D), and because they are constructed to make binary decisions about possibly true/possibly false null hypotheses, psychologists should seriously consider Bayesian statistics. First they compute the probability of T/D, which scientists have always desired. Second, they are unconcerned with accepting or rejecting null hypotheses; and so acceptance or rejection of studies would be based solely upon methodological considerations. Thus, the issue of problematic literatures (like those noted herein) is moot. Bayesian statistics are designed to fix effect sizes (e.g., humans select 32% correct pictures when 25% are expected by chance alone; implementation intentions produce an effect size of $d = .54$, etc.) and completely avoid the problems of accepting or rejecting studies based on the research's outcomes. One can get a good feel for how Bayesian statistics compare with classical statistical techniques from Howard, Maxwell, and Fleming (2000), where multiple data sets are analyzed with Bayesian and classical statistical techniques. Although it is always frustrating to take a step backward, sometimes it is a necessary task for any science. Our hope is that this small step backward will enable psychology to take its next steps forward.

Finally, these conclusions assume that a natural science approach is flawed but improvable (Howard, 1982, 1986). Some in the human science tradition would see the ambition of this series of studies as a "fool's errand," because such thinkers believe the natural science approach is inherently flawed. Be that as it may, this line of studies has helped mainstream psychology to recognize a prevalent flaw in the way it uses Fisherian statistics. It holds hope that psychology might someday become a better science of humans.

REFERENCES

American Psychological Association. (2001). *Publication Manual of the American Psychological Association* (5th ed.). Washington, DC: APA Books.

Bakan, D. (1967). *On method: Toward a reconstruction of psychological method.* San Francisco: Jossey-Bass.

Bem, D. J., & Honorton, C. (1994). Does psi exist? Replicable evidence for a anomalous process of information transfer. *Psychological Bulletin, 115,* 4–18.

Byrd, R. C. (1988). Positive therapeutic effects of intercessory prayer in a coronary care unit population. *Alternative Therapies in Health and Medicine, 3,* 87–90.

Cohen, J. (1969). *Statistical power analysis for the behavioral sciences.* New York: Academic Press.

Duvall, S., & Tweedie, R. (2000). A non-parametric "trim and fill" method of assessing publication bias in meta-analysis. *Journal of the American Statistical Association, 95,* 89–98.

Giorgi, A. (1970). *Psychology as a human science.* New York: Harper & Row.

Giorgi, A. (1992). The idea of human science. *The Humanistic Psychologist, 20,* 202–217.

Gollwitzer, P. M. (1999). Implementation intentions: Strong effects of simple plans. *American Psychologist, 54,* 493–503.

Harris, W. S., Gowda, M., Kolb, J. W., Strychacz, C. P., Vacek, J. L., Jones, P. G., et al. (1999). A randomized, controlled trial of the effects of remote, intercessory prayer on outcomes in patients admitted to the coronary care unit. *Archives of Internal Medicine, 159,* 2273–2278.

Hedges, L. V., & Vevea, J. L. (1996). Estimating effect size under publication bias; Small sample properties and robustness of a random effects selection model. *Journal of Educational and Behavioral Statistics, 21,* 299–332.

Hetland, L. (2000). Listening to music enhances special-temporal reasoning: Evidence for the Mozart effect. *Journal of Aesthetic Education, 34,* 105–148.

Howard, G. S. (1982). Improving methodology via research on research methods. *Journal of Counseling Psychology, 29,* 318–326.

Howard, G. S. (1986). *Dare we develop a human science?* Notre Dame, IN: Academic Publications.

Howard, G. S., & Conway, C. G. (1986). Can there be an empirical science of volitional action? *American Psychologist, 41,* 1241–1251.

Howard, G. S., Hill, T. L., Maxwell, S. E., Baptista, T. M., Farias, M. H., Coelho, C., et al. (2005). *What is wrong with research literatures? And how to make them right.* New Ideas in Psychology (under review).

Howard, G. S., Lau, M., Johnson, I., Johnson, M., Morrow, V., Looman, M., et al. (2005). Should two wrongs make a right? *Review of General Psychology.*

Howard, G. S., Maxwell, S. E., & Fleming, K. J. (2000). The proof of the pudding: An illustration of the relative strengths of null hypothesis, meta-analysis, and Bayesian analysis. *Psychological Methods, 5,* 315–332.

Howard, G. S., Maxwell, S. E., Wiener, R. L., Boynton, K. S. & Rooney, W. M. (1980). Is a behavioral measure the best estimate of behavioral parameters? Perhaps not. *Applied Psychological Measurement, 4,* 63–69.

Howard, G. S., Ralph, K. M., Gulanick, N. A., Maxwell, S. E., Nance, D. W., & Gerber, S. L. (1979). Internal invalidity in pretest–posttest self-report evaluations and a re-evaluation of retrospective pretests. *Applied Psychological Measurement, 3,* 1–23.

Iyengar, S., & Greenhouse, J. B. (1988). Selection models and the file drawer problem. *Statistical Science, 3,* 109–135.

James, W. (1950). *Principles of psychology,* New York: Dover.

Kraemer, H. C., Gardner, C., Brooks, J. O., & Yesavage, J. A. (1998). Advantages of excluding underpowered studies in meta-analysis: Inclusionist versus exclusionist viewpoints. *Psychological Methods, 3,* 23–31.

Lambert, M. J., & Bergin, A. E. (1994). The effectiveness of psychotherapy. In S. Garfield & A. E. Bergin (Eds.), *The handbook of psychotherapy and behavior change* (pp. 143–189). New York: Wiley.

Lau, M., Howard, G. S., Maxwell, S. E., & Venter, A. (2005). A method for settling research controversies: Are humans telepathic. *Psychological Bulletin* (under review).

Macaskill, P., Walter, S., & Irwig, L. (2001). A comparison of methods to detect publication bias in meta-analysis. *Statistics in Medicine, 20,* 641–654.

Mair, J. M. M. (1989). *Between psychology and psychotherapy: The poetics of experience.* London: Routledge.

Meehl, P. E. (1978). Theoretical risks and tabular asterisks: Sir Karl, Sir Ronald and the slow progress of soft psychology. *Journal of Consulting and Clinical Psychology, 46,* 806–834.

Milton, J., & Wiseman, R. (1999). Does psi exist? Lack of replication of an anomalous process of information transfer. *Psychological Bulletin, 125,* 387–391.

Rogers, C. R. (1973). Some new challenges. *American Psychologist, 28,* 379–387.

Rosenthal, R. (1979). The "file drawer problem" and tolerance for null results. *Psychological Bulletin, 86,* 638–641.

Smith, M. L., Glass, G. V., & Miller, T. I. (1980). *The benefits of psychotherapy.* Baltimore, MD: Johns Hopkins University Press.

Storm, L., & Ertel, S. (2001). Does psi exist? Comments on Milton and Wiseman's (1999) meta-analysis of ganzfeld research. *Psychological Bulletin, 127,* 424–433.

Sweeny, R. (2005). A test of the validity of the "Mozart effect." Unpublished Doctoral dissertation, University of Notre Dame, Notre Dame, IN.

Wertz, F. J. (1992). The humanistic movement in psychology: History, celebration and prospectus. *The Humanistic Psychologist, 20*(2&3), 124–476.

AUTHOR NOTE

Edward A. Delgado-Romero is an Associate Professor of Counseling Psychology at the University of Georgia. He received his PhD in counseling psychology from the University of Notre Dame.

George S. Howard is the Morohan Director of the Arts and Letters College Seminar and a Professor of Psychology at the University of Notre Dame. He received his PhD in counseling psychology from Southern Illinois University, Carbondale.

Authors of many books, their most recent collaboration is entitled, *When Things Begin to Go Bad* published by Hamilton Books, Lantham, MD, 2004.

THE HUMANISTIC PSYCHOLOGIST, *33*(4), 305–319

Rigorously Respecting the Person: The Artistic Science of Experiential Personal Constructivism

L. M. Leitner
Psychology Department
Miami University, Oxford, Ohio

This article reviews humanistic critiques of traditional diagnoses, manualized treatments, and randomized controlled trial research. Humanistic psychology must more aggressively elaborate its alternatives to these mainstream approaches if it is to realize its potential as a human science capable of transforming the field. Humanistic alternatives to these approaches are explored in general and discussed specifically within the context of experiential personal constructivism, 1 theoretical approach to humanistic psychology. However, this research agenda could be applied across many humanistic approaches to clinical psychology and, in so doing, make for an intellectually (and empirically) rigorous defense of theories that respect human experience.

All appearances to the contrary, psychology, particularly clinical psychology, is in the midst of a great crisis.[1] On the one hand, researchers spend more time, money, and effort learning ever more about even less. In so doing, they celebrate theories that reductionistically assume that theories are unnecessary as they discover more facts. The field accepts theories that assume that the *Diagnostic and Statistical Manual of Mental Disorders (DSM)-current version* contains (or at least the *DSM-infinity* will contain) the truth about psychopathology, ignoring viewpoints that would suggest that psychopathology cannot be understood outside of theories of person. The profession standardizes around models of care that are based on artificial, reductionistic, often irrelevant, empirically validated treatments, disen-

---

Correspondence should be addressed to L. M. Leitner, Psychology Department, Miami University, 36 Benton Hall, Oxford, OH 45056. E-mail: leitnelm@muohio.edu

[1]This article was originally the Division of Humanistic Psychology Presidential Address given at the 100th Annual Meeting of the American Psychological Association in Chicago, IL in August, 2002.

franchising many practitioners (not to mention decades of good psychotherapy research).

On the other hand, there is an increasing cry urging psychologists to look more closely at the organism that they ought to be most concerned with—the person. Psychology (psyche + logos) should be more concerned with the study of the soul, or at least the mind, instead of solely the brain. Psychopathology (psyche + pathos) can more rightly be seen as being concerned with the suffering and tragedy of the heart and soul, not merely a branch of applied biochemistry. Finally, psychotherapy (psyche + therapos) is based on the noble tradition of witnessing to the suffering of the heart, not manipulating and controlling (either chemically or behaviorally) the symptoms of human despair.

Leitner and Phillips (2003) described this crisis as the immovable object of an increasingly reductionistic and scientistic approach to the field encountering the irresistible force of humans "searching desperately for solutions to questions involving meaning, purpose, and richness in life—something more than merely behaving differently or feeling less" (p. 1). Humanistic psychology is more than caught in the midst of this crisis; it has unique opportunities to revolutionize the study of the psyche. (When I refer to *humanistic psychology* in this article, I am referring to that broad grouping of theories including, but not necessarily limited to, traditional humanistic psychology, existential psychology, constructivist psychology, and transpersonal psychology.) However, psychologists all too often buy into the notion that theories must either be rigorous or respectful (or either scientific or artistic). Such a position leads them to choose respectful artistry over rigorous science, and this choice leaves them vulnerable to critiques of intellectual sloppiness from nonhumanistic colleagues. It is my position that these forced choices are, in fact, arbitrary and constructed, and that good humanistic theory can be rigorous and respectful, scientific and artistic. Further, the integration of these false dichotomies is essential if humanistic psychology (indeed all of psychology) is to survive and grow.

Leitner and Phillips (2003) described ways the immovable object of scientific psychology reified *DSM* diagnoses, manualized treatments, and randomized controlled trial research. We discussed humanistic critiques of these tendencies and outlined specific steps humanistic scholars could take to rigorously and scientifically counter the prevailing zeitgeist. In this article, after summarizing the arguments and steps, I use experiential personal constructivism (Leitner, 1988), an existential/constructivist theory of person, to illustrate the ways that good humanistic theory can be rigorous and respectful. In so doing, I am neither saying that experiential personal constructivism is the only way this work can be done, nor trying to make constructivists out of everyone here today. Rather, I believe that seeing the ways the steps can be applied in one theory may help others use them in other humanistic, existential, and transpersonal approaches. Before beginning, I provide a brief overview of experiential personal constructivism to create a context for the later discussion.

EXPERIENTIAL PERSONAL CONSTRUCTIVISM

Experiential personal constructivism is an elaboration of Kelly's (1991a, 1991b) classic personal construct psychology, and was developed to understand the experiences of more serious personal struggles. Human psychologists see the person as inherently a meaning-making organism, cocreating reality in interaction with the world. I use the term *cocreate* as the world is neither solely an internal construction nor an external given that is discovered. Rather, individuals encounter a real world that is interconnected and constantly unfolding but can only know that world through the meanings they have to engage it. Thus, reality, although present, is a bit "softer" than the realities many psychologists espouse. The role of the psychologist (as therapist and researcher) is to understand the person's experiential reality, not impose particular ways of being on the client or study participant.

Experiential personal constructivism focuses on the joys and travails of interpersonal connection in life. The theory holds that deep interpersonal connections are absolutely necessary for leading a life that is experienced as rich and rewarding (Leitner, 1985). However, such relationships also carry the potential for the experience of terror, in that they can lead to massive invalidations of one's most central personhood. Thus, people are always choosing between great intimacy with another (with the experience of richness yet potential terror) and limiting the depth of contact (with the experience of safety yet emptiness). People's experiences and actions (including the experiences of psychological symptoms) are seen as the current best compromises between the dilemmas of potentially terrifying richness versus safe emptiness. Experiential personal construct psychotherapy focuses on this vital, alive area of the need to connect with, versus the need to retreat from, others.

Although much more can be said about experiential personal constructivism, I think this very brief overview shows its humanistic and existential roots. The person's experience in the world is respected and honored. Relational connection versus distance is focused on. The person is seen as actively creating meanings that frame experience. The person is seen as active, agentic, creative, and future-focused (as opposed to past determined). The therapist (or researcher) respects the lived wisdom of the person, rather than trying to impose reality on the client (or participant). I turn now to the specific issues of diagnosis, manualized treatment, and outcome research.

Humanistic Psychology and Diagnosis

The fetish for the deification (note the "d") of the current edition of the *DSM* (*DSM-IV-TR*; American Psychiatric Association, 2000) has been extensively criticized. These criticisms include, but are not limited to, theoretical, philosophical, empirical, and clinical grounds (e.g., Breggin, 1994; Caplan, 1995; Kirk &

Kutchins, 1992; Kutchins & Kirk, 1997; Levy, 1992). Humanistic psychology has been at the forefront of these criticisms (e.g., Bohart, O'Hara, & Leitner, 1998; Honos-Webb & Leitner, 2001; Kelly, 1991b; Raskin & Epting, 1993; Rogers, 1951; Sauna, 1994; Szasz, 1987; among many others).

However, "if the last 30 years in psychology have proven anything, they have shown that critiquing the *DSM* in the absence of intellectually defensible alternatives does nothing to change its dominance over the field of human distress" (Leitner & Phillips, 2003, p. 160). Ironically, the idea that humanistic psychologists do not diagnose clients is one of the great myths about humanistic psychology. Many psychologists, including many humanistic psychologists, accept this myth precisely because of the reification of the *DSM*. Diagnosis gets equated with a *DSM* diagnosis; it is not seen as a professional understanding of the client by the therapist from within the therapist's theoretical framework. Both classic (e.g., Becker, 1973; Bugental, 1999; Kelly, 1991a, 1991b, Maslow, 1970; Moustakas, 1975; Perls, Hefferline, & Goodman, 1951; Rogers, 1951; Yalom, 1980) and more current (e. g. Greenberg, Rice, & Elliott, 1993; Leitner, Faidley, & Celentana, 2000; Wilbur, 1984) humanistic psychologists diagnose persons they engage in therapy, although the diagnosis given may have little, if anything, to do with the *DSM*. (See Leitner & Phillips, 2003, for a more thorough discussion of this issue.)

Let me illustrate using a diagnostic system within experiential personal constructivism (Leitner, Faidley, & Celentana, 2000). This system consists of three axes. First, there is an axis that assesses whether the development of the construction of self and other has been arrested due to severe trauma (see Faidley, 2001). Intimate relationships are extremely chaotic if one cannot be clear about where one ends and the other begins, as well as have a felt sense of the other's presence and constancy over time. The second axis is an assessment of the person's interpersonal style. For example, people may disperse their dependency needs in ways that either facilitate or hinder deep human contact. Finally, there is an experiential axis on which people can be assessed in terms of their relational struggles based on a constructivist perspective on optimal functioning (Leitner & Pfenninger, 1994).

Although humanistic psychology has elaborated many creative ways of understanding human distress, "creative theory does not a diagnostic system make" (Leitner & Phillips, 2003, p. 162). If one truly wants to dislodge the *DSM* from its hegemony over the field, one must show that these alternative positions are in fact better than the *DSM*. This means, of course, that one must do research. Many humanistic psychologists seem opposed to research because the term has been literalistically equated with a particular reductionistic method. Bakan (1967) termed this worship of a specific method "methodalatry." Psychologists must recapture the term so that *research* becomes the systematic gaining of evidence evaluating a position (Leitner & Phillips, 2003). As I discuss the following points, I will suggest quantitative and qualitative research projects that illustrate some of the points mentioned.

Leitner and Phillips (2003, p. 163) urged humanistic psychologists to systematically evaluate diagnostic systems using the following template:

- Develop clear descriptors of the humanistic diagnostic terms to be studied, complete with illustrative examples. These descriptors may need to be revised and re-revised based on input from practicing therapists until a satisfactory level of clarity has been reached.
- Assess whether different therapists can agree on the use of the system with illustrative cases. Again, the descriptors and examples may need to be revised and re-revised until a satisfactory level of intertherapist agreement has been reached.
- Compare the humanistic diagnostic understanding to the traditional nosology. Which system is more helpful to therapists and to clients? Which system gives the client the most hope and makes the client feel empathically respected?

Develop clear descriptors.   Obviously, to systematically study phenomena, one must have clear descriptors of them. (I am arguing for clarity, not necessarily reductionism, two terms that get confused in practice.) For example, *discrimination*, one of the components of the experiential axis in experiential personal constructivism, has been defined as the ability to construe differences between self and other, and evaluate the impact those differences will have on the self (Leitner & Pfenninger, 1994). Discrimination is a major issue when choosing whether to risk the potential terror of intimate relationships. It would be easy to have therapists rate the clarity of the description, as well as have them give feedback as to why it is not as clear as it could be (see the Appendix).

Comparing to the current nosology.   Once one has descriptors that are clear and that therapists can use reliably, one already is far beyond the *DSM*. One then could compare a humanistic diagnostic system to the *DSM*. For example, one could provide written descriptions of clients based on their experiential constructivist diagnoses, as well as their *DSM* diagnoses, to the clients and their therapists. Table 1 shows some questions that could be asked for any humanistic conceptualization system.

In this study, the psychologist would not be asking for any objective TRUTHS. Rather, he is assessing the degree to which each system of understanding human distress has treatment implications, instills hope, makes the client feel respected, and so on. In other words, in true humanistic fashion, the psychologist is assessing the ways these conceptualizations are helpful to clients. In his concept of transitive diagnosis, Kelly (1991b) argued that a system, no matter how accurately it describes a client's struggles, is useless unless it also points to options for growth, change, development, or elaboration.

TABLE 1
Examples of Questions

The questions below could be asked of case descriptions based upon the DSM and any humanistic system. These are illustrative questions.

1. Please rate how accurately you believe the case description describes your client's struggles.
2. Please rate the extent to which the case description helps you understand your client.
3. Please rate the extent to which the case description increased your ability to feel for the client.
4. Please rate the extent to which the case description helped you see strengths in the client that you might otherwise have overlooked.
5. Please rate the extent to which the case description makes you feel optimistic about the client's chances for improvement.

All of these could be rated on a scale like the one below:

1	2	3	4	5	6	7
not at all		slightly		moderately		extremely

Note.   Clients will complete similar questions about the case descriptions and their experience of themselves and the therapy process.

(As an aside, I recently submitted an unsuccessful National Institute of Mental Health grant application to do exactly this project. A major reason it was turned down was because questions about which conceptualization inspires more hope, makes the client feel more respected, and so on were seen by the reviewers as too biased against the *DSM* system to be a fair test. I do not know whether this is humorous aside, a tragic aside, or even if it really is an aside.)

Qualitative research also could be done to explore, in a more in depth fashion, the experience of being diagnosed within the alternate systems. What does it feel like to be seen in that particular way? Why does it feel that way? What effect did it have on the relationship with the therapist to know that the therapist was viewing the client in a given way? These are just a few of the questions that could be answered through qualitative investigations of the experience of diagnosis.

Humanistic Psychology and Manualized Treatments

When I speak of the manualization of treatments, I am referring to the movement to specify what occurs within therapy sessions, as opposed to evaluating the effectiveness of a therapy across sessions. Manualization of treatments is tied to the belief that, if one can eliminate the variability of the person of the therapist (through having all therapists do the same thing), one can have uniform and consistent treatments, much like medicine. The threat of manualization of treatments to the profession of humanistic psychology is well known (see Bohart, O'Hara, & Leitner, 1998, for a review). Manualization assumes that therapy is something someone does to another, not a creative encounter with another. Therapy "can be manually described or prescribed no more than the connection between two lovers on a romantic evening" (Leitner & Phillips, 2003, p. 164). I propose creative therapeutic artistry as an alternative to manualization (see Bohart, 2001).

However, creative artistry should not be confused with an "anything goes" approach to therapy. Although art cannot be studied reductionistically, people can determine that Rembrandt had much more painting talent than Leitner ever will. Psychologists must be able to evaluate the therapeutic encounter if they are to distinguish between better and worse therapy. In other words, therapeutic creativity is not merely the development of novel ways of understanding and approaching clients. (Trust me, my way of drawing a portrait would be novel.) There are principles underlying the creative encounter with the client. Let me illustrate with fine cooking. The French developed *nouvelle cuisine* as a way of using the underlying principles of cooking to approach food in new and creative ways. The principles themselves had to be understood and mastered prior to moving to *nouvelle cuisine* (Dornenburg & Page, 1996). Returning to the therapy room, the principles underlying the encounter with the client can be tested to distinguish those that are creative versus merely strange.

Humanistic psychologists place great credibility on the client's lived experience. Based on this principle, Leitner and Guthrie (1993) argued that any therapeutic intervention can be seen as either affirmed or disconfirmed by client experience. An intervention is confirmed to the extent that the client experiences life as richer and more meaningful, the relationship with the therapist becomes more meaningful, the client brings new material into the therapy, and the client's level of distress changes (Leitner & Guthrie, 1993). When interventions do not lead to these client experiences, the therapist should question whether the intervention (and the principles underlying the intervention) is a creative act or merely the therapist's own weirdness. In other words, interventions that are affirmed by the client may be creative; those that are disconfirmed are the therapists' failures to relate (Honos-Webb & Leitner, 2002). This approach to validation of therapist interventions empowers the client to codetermine the direction and outcome of therapy, and is tremendously therapeutic (Leitner, 2001). It also empowers the client to experientially validate treatment versus the mainstream empirically validated treatment (EVT) approach. In other words, we have our own version of EVTs! (Or, if you prefer the wolf in sheep's clothing terminology, experientially supported treatments [ESTs].)

Leitner and Phillips (2003) proposed the following program of scholarship to understand the importance of true therapeutic artistry:

- Develop and clarify principles underlying humanistic artistic encounters. If necessary, revise and re-revise until an acceptable level of clarity is reached.
- Confirm, through client experience, that encounters based on these principles actually benefit clients. Be prepared to discard principles that do not lead to encounters that can be shown to benefit clients.
- Use client experience to compare encounters based on these principles to manualized techniques.

TABLE 2
Validation and Invalidation of Interventions

Therapy Event	Validational Inference
1. Client experiences life as richer and more meaningful	Validation
Client experiences life as less meaningful	Invalidation
2. Connection between therapist and client deepens	Validation
Connection stagnates, shallows, or disrupts	Invalidation
3. Client brings new material into therapy	Validation
No new material, ruminating over past material	Invalidation
4. Symptoms change	Validation
No change	Invalidation
Underlying Principles for Inferring Validation or Invalidation	
1. When all indicators point toward validation	Powerful affirmation
2. When all indicators point toward invalidation	Powerful disconfirmation
3. When indicators are "mixed" rely most strongly on the connection between therapist and client indicator (#2)	
4. When being invalidated, the therapist should reassess and determine why he or she is not grasping the client's experience.	

Develop and clarify principles. As with diagnostic descriptors, these underlying principles need to be clear if they are to be systematically investigated. For example, the Leitner and Guthrie (1993) description of when an intervention is validated versus invalidated can be used to represent one set of principles within experiential personal construct psychotherapy (see Table 2).

Compare to manualized techniques. Although the assessment of Principles 1 and 2 may seem straightforward (or even trite), providing client experiential evidence that these indicators are, in fact, ways clients say they are benefiting from therapy sets the stage for more definitive work. For example, does a therapy that pays careful attention to client experiences of validation and invalidation result in more instances of powerful affirmation (and fewer instances of powerful disconfirmation) than a manualized treatment where such experiences are less central? When getting ambiguous validational material from the client, do manualized therapists pay less attention to the therapy relationship indicator as the most important criterion for determining whether therapy is on track? Do therapists following these principles correct their understandings and interventions when the client disconfirms them more than therapists practicing some manualized technique? If so, are such therapies experienced as more powerful and helpful by clients than the manualized treatments extant in the field today? Are manualized therapies that are successful, in fact, violating the treatment manual at times when the therapy is in trouble to focus on the relationship and save the therapy, as some critics have suggested (Brooke, 2002)? What a line of scholarship, all based on one set of principles from one humanistic theory of therapy! At this point, psychologists would have empirical support for experientially supported treatments (ESEST), one-upping the EST folks!

Humanistic Psychology and Double Blind Outcome Studies

Tied closely to the manualized treatment movement, psychology has attempted to adopt randomized controlled trials (RCTs) as the gold standard of outcome studies (as well as what therapies should be taught in high quality training programs). The hidden assumptions behind the privileging of RCTs have been documented, and the ways those assumptions bias the field toward cognitive, behavioral, and chemical interventions detailed (Bohart et al., 1998; Leitner & Phillips, 2003; Task Force for the Development of Guidelines for the Provision of Humanistic Psychosocial Services, 1997). However, critiquing the dominant view without providing solid evidence supporting some alternative leaves humanistic psychologists vulnerable to the view that they are avoiding answering legitimate questions about psychotherapy (e.g., Do these therapies work? Why? Are there approaches to humanistic therapy that are not useful to clients? etc.).

Ironically, the RCT movement also erroneously discredits decades of good psychotherapy outcome research, including good outcome research on humanistic therapies. Carl Rogers (e.g., Rogers & Dymond, 1954) is widely regarded as one of the very first psychologist to systematically evaluate his approach to therapy. Further, recent meta-analyses (e.g., Elliott, 1996; Greenberg, Elliott, & Liataer, 1994; Viney, 1998) show strong support for the efficacy of humanistic and constructivist therapies, even using quantitative models of assessing efficacy. Rennie (2002) reviewed numerous qualitative studies supporting humanistic therapies. (See Cain & Seeman, 2002, for a thorough review of this research.)

In other words, humanistic scholars already have provided quantitative and qualitative data on the efficacy of humanistic therapies. These scholars are, then, facing a tremendous opportunity. If they follow up on this research by systematically exploring the reasons nonmanualized yet technically clear therapies work, they have the opportunity to place their approaches to human suffering on the same level as the mainstream positions. In this context, Leitner and Phillips (2003, p. 169) suggested the following template to guide further research into the outcome of humanistic psychotherapy (vs. the within session research referred to earlier):

- Clearly specify and illustrate the bases of each approach to humanistic psychotherapy. If necessary, revise and re-revise these illustrations until an acceptable level of clarity is reached.
- Use qualitative and quantitative studies to determine the effectiveness of the utilization of these principles.

Clearly specify and illustrate bases of humanistic therapies.   Each humanistic therapy can detail the bases of its approach to the client. For example, one of the bases of experiential personal construct psychotherapy is the importance of the experience of paradoxical safety in the therapy relationship (Leitner, 2001). If the therapist is successful in creating a safe place (Havens, 1989), the client begins to struggle with revealing the most personally threatening material. Thus, because therapy is safe, the client risks more and, paradoxically, feels threatened about whether the safety of the therapy room will still hold. (I believe this is similar to what Perls, 1965, referred to as the "safe emergency" of the therapy room in the famous Gloria tapes.)

Please note that, although paradoxical safety is clear and precise as a concept, it does not mandate specific interventions. In other words, therapists may use innumerable specific techniques to implement paradoxical safety. However, by having the concept clearly specified, therapists and researchers can assess whether a given therapist–client dyad achieved this goal. In so doing, they can systematically investigate the concept.

Investigate the effectiveness of these approaches.   Using paradoxical safety as an example, therapists could ask clients many questions at the end of therapy. They could ask whether they felt safe in the therapy. They could ask whether that sense of safety seemed important to the client. They could ask whether the safety made them more likely to reveal important and potentially distressing experiences to the therapist. They also could ask about the helpfulness of the therapy. They could determine the extent to which paradoxical safety was experienced in successful nonhumanistic therapies, implying that humanistic relational principles were operating in these therapies. Again, questions such as these could be addressed quantitatively, qualitatively, or in both ways.

When these types of questions are combined with questions around other components of experiential personal construct psychotherapy (e.g., optimal therapeutic distance, therapist trusting and respecting the client, therapist hope, genuineness, etc.), researchers have the opportunity to understand the ways that a therapy relationship needs to be structured to benefit the client. They have ways of evaluating whether a therapist is failing a client. They have ways of discarding components that clients say are not relevant. In this way, therapists can become technically clear and extremely specific about therapy without prescribing specific behaviors. In my opinion, this would provide the scholarly foundations for true therapeutic creativity.

IN CONCLUSION

I hope this article has shown that humanistic, existential, constructivist, and transpersonal psychologies have a historically unique opportunity. Practitioners have the chance to do more than defend the all too limited turf of respecting the human in psychology. They have the opportunity to show the field that the human can be respectfully engaged in systematic scholarship. They have the chance to show what a truly holistic approach (integrating heart and head, soma and psyche) can do for enriching the lives of people.

However, to truly realize the potential described here, humanist psychologists must do one more thing—they must start placing more humanistically oriented professors in mainstream colleges and universities. If they fail to increase the number of humanistically oriented professors, students will have limited opportunity to discover the exciting work being done. The net result will be increasing marginalization, despite the brilliance of the scholarship. The profession will become increasingly sterile, and future clients and therapists will suffer (Orlinsky, Botermas, & Ronnestad, 2001). Therefore, let me propose the following agenda to increase the representation of humanistic psychologists in the academy:

- Undergraduates who are interested in humanistic psychology can be surveyed to determine their views on the advantages and disadvantages of faculty life. If appropriate, misconceptions can be clarified.
- Humanistic faculty at mainstream universities can volunteer to teach research methods from a humanistic perspective.
- Undergraduates interested in humanistic psychology should be encouraged to explore and perform humanistic scholarship. This will do more than make them competitive with traditional students who already are doing traditional research; it also will let them see first-hand how exciting humanistic scholarship can be.
- Humanistic faculty at mainstream graduate programs should try to insure that some of each year's admitting class are humanistically oriented.
- Humanistic faculty should attempt to publish research in mainstream journals. Although the rejection rates are brutal, even the occasional published piece raises the profile of humanistic psychology in the field.
- Humanistic graduate professors should routinely work on publications with these interested graduate students. This makes the future professional more competitive for an academic job and teaches the student the many issues and approaches to publication.
- APA Division 32 should systematically seek out and mentor new faculty members who are humanistically oriented.

As the field faces these immovable objects, practitioners can see opportunities that only humanistic psychology can engage. Let me conclude by quoting from Leitner and Phillips (2003, p. 169) one more time:

> As our existential colleagues will remind us, we always have a choice. Currently, we can choose to drown in the tidal wave of reductionistic thought or we can seize the

moment to transform the field. Further, our existential colleagues would push us to realize that we are responsible for the consequences of that choice. If we choose poorly, we have no one to blame but ourselves. However, if we choose wisely and well, being aggressive pursuing our ideas while also being open to evidence, in a few generations psychology may become what it was intended to become—the investigation of the profound mysteries of the human heart and soul.

I thank you for your attention to these thoughts today. I thank you for the honor of having allowed me to be your president.

REFERENCES

American Psychiatric Association. (2000). *Diagnostic and statistical manual of mental disorders* (4th ed.). Washington, DC: Author.

Bakan, D. (1967). *On method: Toward a reconstruction of psychological investigation.* San Francisco: Jossey-Bass.

Becker, E. (1973). *Denial of Death.* New York: Free Press.

Bohart, A. C. (2001, August). *The therapist as improvisational artist.* Paper presented at the annual meeting of the American Psychological Association, San Francisco, CA.

Bohart, A. C., O'Hara, M., & Leitner, L. M. (1998). Empirically violated treatments: Disenfranchisement of humanistic and other psychotherapies. *Psychotherapy Research, 8,* 141–157.

Breggin, P. (1994). *Toxic psychiatry.* New York: St. Martin's Press.

Brooke, R. (2002, July). *From metaphors of war to metaphors of hospitality: A Jungian alternative to empirically supported treatments.* Paper presented at the IAAP Academic Conference on Analytical Psychology, Colchester, UK.

Bugental, J. F. T. (1999). *Psychotherapy isn't what you think.* Phoenix, AZ: Zeig, Tucker.

Cain, D. J., & Seeman, J. (Eds.). (2002). *Humanistic psychotherapies: Handbook of research and practice.* Washington, DC: American Psychological Association.

Caplan, P. J. (1995). *They say you're crazy: How the world's most powerful psychiatrists decide who's normal: The inside story of the DSM.* New York: Addison-Wesley.

Dornenburg, A., & Page, K. (1996). *Culinary artistry.* New York: Wiley

Elliott, R. (1996). Are client-centered/experiential therapies effective? A meta-analysis of outcome research. In U. Esser, H. Pabst, & G. W. Speierer (Eds.), *The power of the person-centered approach: New challenges, perspectives, answers* (pp. 125–138). Köln, Germany: GwG Verlag.

Faidley, A. J. (2001). "You've been like a mother to me:" Treatment implications of nonverbal knowing and developmental arrest. *The Humanistic Psychologist, 29,* 138–166.

Greenberg, L. S., Elliott, R., & Liataer, G. (1994). Research on humanistic and experiential psychotherapies. In A. E. Bergin & S. L. Garfield (Eds.), *Handbook of psychotherapy and behavior change* (4th ed., pp. 509–539). New York: Wiley.

Greenberg, L. S., Rice, L. N., & Elliott, R. (1993). *Facilitating emotional change.* New York: Guilford Press.

Havens, L. L. (1989). *A safe place: Laying the groundwork of psychotherapy.* Cambridge, MA: Harvard University Press.

Honos-Webb, L., & Leitner, L. M. (2001). How using the *DSM* causes damage: A client's report. *Journal of Humanistic Psychology, 41,* 4, 34–54.

Honos-Webb, L., & Leitner, L. M. (2002). Therapy case formulation as interventional assessment. *The Humanistic Psychologist, 30,* 102–113.

Kelly, G. A. (1991a). *The psychology of personal constructs (Vol. 1): A theory of personality.* London: Routledge. (Original work published 1955)

Kelly, G. A. (1991b). *The psychology of personal constructs (Vol. 2): Clinical diagnosis and psychotherapy.* London: Routledge. (Original work published 1955.)

Kirk, S., & Kutchins, H. (1992). *The selling of DSM: The rhetoric of science in psychiatry.* New York: Aldine & DeGruyter.

Kutchins, H., & Kirk, S. A. (1997). *DSM: The psychiatric bible and the creation of mental disorders.* New York: Free Press.

Leitner, L. M. (1985). The terrors of cognition: On the experiential validity of personal construct theory. In D. Bannister (Ed.), *Issues and approaches in personal construct theory* (pp. 83–103). London: Academic.

Leitner, L. M. (1988). Terror, risk, & reverence: Experiential personal construct psychotherapy. *International Journal of Personal Construct Psychology, 1,* 261–272.

Leitner, L. M. (2001). Experiential personal construct therapeutic artistry: The therapy relationship and the timing of interventions. *The Humanistic Psychologist, 29,* 98–113.

Leitner, L. M., Faidley, A. J., & Celentana, M. A. (2000). Diagnosing human meaning making: An experiential constructivist approach. In R. A. Neimeyer & J. D. Raskin (Eds.), *Constructions of disorder: Meaning-making frameworks for psychotherapy* (pp. 175–204). American Psychological Association: Washington, DC.

Leitner, L. M., & Guthrie, A. J. (1993). Validation of therapist interventions in psychotherapy: Clarity, ambiguity, subjectivity. *International Journal of Personal Construct Psychology, 6,* 281–135.

Leitner, L. M., & Pfenninger, D. T. (1994). Sociality and optimal functioning. *Journal of Constructivist Psychology, 7,* 119–135.

Leitner, L. M., & Phillips, S. (2003). The immovable object versus the irresistible force: Problems and opportunities for humanistic psychology. *Journal of Humanistic Psychology, 43,* 156–173.

Levy, D. (1992). A proposed category for the *Diagnostic and Statistical Manual of Mental Disorders (DSM)*: Pervasive labeling disorder. *Journal of Humanistic Psychology, 32,* 121–125.

Maslow, A. H. (1970). *Motivation and personality.* New York: Harper & Row.

Moustakas, C. E. (1975). *Who will listen?* New York: Norton.

Orlinsky, D. E., Botermas, J. F., Ronnestad, M. H. (2001). Towards an empirically grounded model of psychotherapy training: Four thousand therapists rate influences on their development. *Australian Psychologist, 36,* 139–148.

Perls, F. (1965). *Three approaches to psychotheraphy: Number 2: Dr. Frederick Perls.* New York: Psychological Films, Inc.

Perls, F. S., Hefferline, R. F., & Goodman, P. (1951). *Gestalt therapy: Excitement and growth in the human personality.* New York: Julian Press.

Raskin, J. D., & Epting, F. R. (1993). Personal construct theory and the argument against mental illness. *International Journal of Personal Construct Psychology, 6,* 351–369.

Rennie, D. L. (2002). Experiencing psychotherapy: Grounded theory studies. In D. J. Cain & J. Seeman (Eds.), *Humanistic psychotherapies: Handbook of research and practice* (pp. 117–144). Washington, DC: American Psychological Association.

Rogers, C. R. (1951). *Client-centered therapy.* Boston: Houghton Mifflin.

Rogers, C. R., & Dymond, R. F. (Eds.). (1954). *Psychotherapy and personality change.* Chicago: University of Chicago Press.

Sauna, V. D. (1994). Quo Vidis APA? Inroads of the medical model. *The Humanistic Psychologist, 18,* 85–89.

Szasz, T. (1987). *Insanity: The idea and its consequences.* New York: Wiley.

Taskforce for the Development of Guidelines for the Provision of Humanistic Psychosocial Services. (1997). Guidelines for the provision of humanistic psychosocial services. *The Humanistic Psychologist, 25,* 64–107.

Viney, L. L. (1998). Should we use personal construct therapy? A paradigm for outcomes evaluation. *Psychotherapy: Theory, research, practice, training, 35,* 366–380.

Wilbur, K. (1984). The developmental spectrum and psychopathology: Treatment modalities. *Journal of Transpersonal Psychology, 16,* 137–166.

Yalom, I. (1980). *Existential psychotherapy.* New York: Basic Books.

APPENDIX 1
DESCRIPTION OF DISCRIMINATION

Discrimination: the ability to construe differences between self and other and evaluate the impact those differences will have on you.

People can struggle with discrimination in many ways. First, people may underdiscriminate by having difficulty seeing the ways that others are different from them. Struggles in this area often can be seen by the person assuming that others feel the same way about issues, value the same things, like the same people, etc. For example, Patricia, referred for therapy due to "panic attacks," would disclose intimate details of her life to most everyone she would meet. She did not bother to evaluate whether these people might potentially be injuring to her due to differences in their experiences of the world versus hers.

People may be able to see differences between self and other, yet err on the side of assuming such differences are manageable and will not adversely affect the ongoing relationship. For example, a client had a long history of falling in love with whomever he happened to be dating. When the romantic partner would raise concerns about the viability of the potential relationship, he would argue that the differences being expressed could be worked out "if we love one another enough." He had great difficulty in differentiating between differences that might add spice and zest to the relationship and those that might lead to a high likelihood of devastating injuries.

Struggles with overdiscrimination also can be seen in two ways. First, people may struggle with seeing any ways that others are like them. Struggles of this nature often can be seen through the experience of surprise when others feel the same way about issues, value the same things, or like the same people. The predominance of the experience of being different from others, unable to connect, or viewing the world in uniquely different ways may also be a manifestation of struggles in this area. For example, a client can be invested in contrasting his or her ways of experiencing the world from the "mundane" and "middle class" ways of others.

People also can struggle with overdiscrimination through the process of inferring excessive risks and dangers associated with the differences they do see between themselves and other people. Perceived differences lead to the experience of potential betrayal and injury. For example, William, referred for therapy for depression, had difficulty talking about the intimate details of his life due to his fears over what the other might do with the information. He was quite worried about the others "gossiping" about him and telling people he did not know about potentially embarrassing details of life.

AUTHOR NOTE

Larry M. Leitner is a Professor of Psychology at Miami University in Oxford, Ohio. He is a Fellow in the American Psychological Association and a past President of the Division of Humanistic Psychology. His scholarship focuses on the applicability of experiential constructivism to conceptualize and therapeutically engage persons struggling with severe pathology.

THE HUMANISTIC PSYCHOLOGIST, 33(4), 321–334

Humanistic Research in the Wake of Postmodernism

Scott D. Churchill

Department of Psychology
University of Dallas

Talk about "ways of knowing" currently takes place in an arena that more and more looks upon such epistemologies skeptically. Humanistic, as well as postmodern traditions acknowledge the relativities of perception, which extend, of course, to the realm of scientific investigation and discourse. Theoretical and even methodological values that humanist psychologists hold dear can be shown, on reflection, to have a foundation in their individual biographies. What does it mean, then, to strive for truthful understanding in humanistic research? The epistemological question is: to what do people's linguistic acts refer—to "real" experiences, to other linguistic acts, to personal values? Postmodernism suggests that the answer to this question would be the chain of signifiers that make up people's knowledge systems, whereas humanistic psychology (in its "phenomenological" adumbration) maintains a relational bond between the chain of signifiers and the situations that are signified (between the *expressions* of psychological life and the *experiences* to which those expressions refer)—as well as between linguistic acts and personal values. After placing humanistic phenomenology into dialogue with postmodern challenges, this article explores the nature of psychological data and knowledge, asking if there is a "reality base" for research beyond the chains of signifiers that constitute both the data and analyses of qualitative research. What is the "reality status" of the situations that serve as ground and purpose for psychological research?

I

The first half of the 20th Century saw the rise of humanism in academic and professional psychology, as well as in the field of psychiatry. For a while, the medical model gave way to myth and metaphor as Freud's work led to that of Jung, Adler,

---

Correspondence should be addressed to Scott D. Churchill, 1845 East Northgate Drive, Irving, TX 75062. E-mail: bonobo@udallas.edu

Reich, and eventually to the interpersonal and humanistic schools. In the field of philosophy, Husserl's transcendental aims were subverted by Heidegger, Sartre, Merleau-Ponty, and Levinas (among others) into more human-centered and historically situated concerns. Value-laden understandings of the human self gave rise simultaneously to the American humanistic psychologists' preoccupation with self-actualization, to European philosophers' notions regarding authentic "being one's self," and even to contemporary Eastern psychology's emphasis on self-forgetfulness. Then postmodernism came along and began exposing the political underpinnings as well as the epistemological tenuousness of the many divergent assertions about reality that have emerged (Derrida, 1967/1973, 1967/1976; Foucault, 1969/1976, 1980). So where does the field stand now?

Terms such as *truth* and *self* no longer seem viable in the wake of postmodernism, as such language appears to lay claim to impossible essences and unities. In their place there are only contingencies and disunities. What is left to do, for the old-school humanistic and existential phenomenologists who once offered a light at the end of the tunnel, who found ways of acknowledging a "multiverse" (and not simply a "universe") of ideas, yet stood on the firm ground of their convictions regarding ontologically revealed "depth dimensions" of human reality? When, in 1949, Heidegger (1949/1956) wrote his essay entitled "The Way Back into the Ground of Metaphysics," he seemed to be offering up something solid on which to stand, indeed, a perspective that could "understand" everything else. The image he offered was that of a tree, sinking its (metaphysical) roots into solid (ontological) ground, extending its (disciplinary) branches into the sky. What happens when this whole scheme is turned upside down, and seemingly vanishes into thin air after a wave of the Derridian wand?

Many psychologists today find themselves situated somewhere between the assuring certitudes of their formative years, and the not so assuring challenges coming from the forward edge of collective intellectual history. At such times, one pauses, reflects, and takes stock. This article is the result of one such taking stock, in which a humanistic psychologist enters into a self-critical examination of his own values, and asks, with a searching eye, "What among the rich ideas of my formative years can still hold true for me today? How do I think, teach, and continue to grow in light of the healthy skepticism introduced to me via postmodern thought?"

In a way, this project was, at its inception, an effort to "fess up" to my humanistic and existential value commitments, and then to apologize for them. I say this a bit facetiously; but the truth is, everyone needs to engage in a bit of self-examination from time to time. Alas, I have not done very well here because, in the end, I found myself unable to uproot my values and fundamental principles as a humanistic psychologist. Instead of Grand Narratives deprived of their grandness, what I found were enduring convictions grounded in many years of mentoring qualitative research projects from within a humanistic framework. In reflecting on the issues raised in my opening paragraphs, I realize that part of being human is having a history; and that this history cannot be undone or simply taken out of play via deconstruction. I further realize that, rather than apologize, I prefer to celebrate the lived hermeneutic by which the notions communicated to me by my college and graduate school professors have become my own.

My first exposure to existential philosophy was in 1969, when I had just been issued a draft number of 99 (at the time, a not so comforting thought) in the first citizens' draft ever for the Vietnam War. In the same year, I was introduced to many new experiences (yes, I did inhale), and was blown away by the new ideas I was learning. I can recall admiring my college professors, wanting to be like them, yearning to understand the deeper meaning of philosophers such as Jaspers, Heidegger, Sartre, and Camus. Everything that characterizes who I was at that point in my life, at that very point in history—all of this is the backdrop against which I assimilated the ideas that would become my destiny to profess and to continue reflecting on. Indeed, it would be an interesting exercise (in terms of our own professed principles of hermeneutics) to juxtapose the texts that individuals read as undergraduate and graduate students with the events that were taking place in their lives, at the time they were reading them. And I would argue that it is the spirit of my times, and not, for example, that of Husserl's or Heidegger's, that lie at the basis of the values and existential concepts that I hold dear.

I cannot pretend to really know the political context within which Heidegger (1927/1962) wrote *Being and Time*, or within which Sartre (1943/1956) wrote *Being and Nothingness*—even if I might inform myself about their meaning and motivational contexts. The fact remains that my own understanding of these thinkers belongs to my biography, not theirs. (When I, as a teacher, present Freud or Sartre or whomever in class, it is not Freud or Sartre that gets communicated to my students. Rather, it is my personal understanding of whomever I am presenting.) In retrospect, I can say that I was ready for a personal absorption of existential philosophy at that time in my life. Heidegger believed "a readiness must be there" before one steps into the path of phenomenology (1923/2005, p. 1). I may have been only 18 years old when I first read Heidegger, but I can still remember the awe I experienced when my first Heidegger teacher would refer in class to "Being with a capital B." This was my first introduction to the ontological difference. (Those of us who were the newly initiated would playfully call each other "Dasein," as if we belonged to a secret society.) In college and then in graduate school, Heidegger's *existentialia* were discussed not only in class, but in hallways, in all night "bull sessions," even in crowded bars. We were incorporating our reading of Heidegger into our understanding—our understanding—of what it meant to be human, of what it meant to be studying existential phenomenology in America in the early Seventies. And when, in my current life, I teach Heidegger, it is certainly not an interest in National Socialism that animates my teaching, but rather the wonderful revelations of my college days, the spirit of my times, that I find myself communicating.

This is likewise true when I teach qualitative research. Here I am drawing on not only the wisdom of my teachers—Paul Colaizzi, Rolf von Eckartsberg, William

Fischer, Amedeo Giorgi—but even more so on the very personal way that I internalized their teachings, along with the teachings of my clinical mentors (Constance Fischer, Charles Maes, and Anthony Barton). I tell my students that I am teaching them what my teachers taught me. I instruct them to cite the writings of my teachers as their sources. My own natural attitude here is my belief that what I know (and teach) is precisely what my teachers taught me, as though I were a blank slate or sieve through which their teachings were simply passed on to my students. Of course, what I present to my students is my own unique synthesis of what my teachers taught me, of what I have read in books, and of how I integrate all this within my own personal experience. I realize now that if I were to deconstruct what I teach to my students, this would probably be less a matter of revealing hidden power assumptions imported from the authors I have read, and more a matter of revealing my own psychological interests, dreams, and yes, blind spots. Perhaps one reason I have tended to keep postmodernism at an arm's length is that I am still enjoying the process of passionately living out my own "personal myth," as one of my teachers, Father Murray, used to call it. (I can hear the Lacanian in the background saying "enjoy your symptom!" There is, indeed, a *jouissance* involved in teaching, and I suspect that if my academic life were to be subjected to deconstruction, it would be Lacan rather than Foucault who would be the most illuminating of my own particular blind spots.)

What I wish to communicate here is the very personal nature of what people call *knowledge*. In this regard, I tend to agree more with Kierkegaard than with postmodernists regarding the source and origins of our thoughts and values. Yes, I have incorporated the latter from out of the social world; but they bear my indelible stamp. I have taken them up, and made them my own—just as patients and research participants have made certain "social constructs" about their psychological lives their own. Thus, as a phenomenologically trained humanistic researcher, if I am to understand the meanings of the words, thoughts, and values of my research participants, it is not going to be to the social history texts that I turn, but rather to research interviews with the participants themselves, to find out precisely what their narratives mean to them.

What, in essence, concerns me the most about postmodern psychology is the resulting loss of the depth dimensions of the psychological subject. Individuals are no longer selves with souls, but rather agents (or pawns) who merely activate a sense of self. The *whence* and *whither* of human being do not stand in existential relation when that being now refers to one's (displaced?) place in an endless chain of signifiers. Is this not one of the ambiguities that Heidegger (1927/1962) guarded against with his notion of the "care structure"[1]—the idea that one's ownmost projects, one's authentic possibilities, and even one's average everydayness are all exi-

---

[1]With respect to Heidegger's care structure, in which the temporal ecstasies of past (facticity, thrownness, attunement), present (fallenness, circumspective concern, discourse) and future (existence, projection, understanding) are ontologically interdependent and equiprimordial, one finds in traditional and postmodern psychology variations in which one moment within this existential

stentially rooted in the historical (and biographical) situation within which one finds oneself? For Heidegger, this "facticity"[2]—this relation to a situation into which one is "thrown"—is not a hapless relation to grand narratives and social constructions, but rather a very personal way in which one embodies one's "founding" [*Fundierung*], and in which one initiates one's own way of "bodying-forth" [*leiben*] and thereby "saying" (if only in silence) something special and personal about the meaning of one's being. This is why the existentially trained psychologist is engaged in "hearkening"[3] (and not just processing data or reframing narratives).

Indeed, as I have presented elsewhere (Churchill, 2002), the aim of "narrative therapy in the postmodern world," as described by Parry and Doan (1994) is "to

---

gestalt is given undue priority. With traditional psychology, there is a totalization of *thrownness*, so that all one can see is determinism. This is expressed and symbolized by the equation $y = f(x)$, which states that behavior (y) is simply a function of antecedent variables (x). With that equal sign (in which the present is reduced to the past) no room is left for choice (future projection). With postmodernism, there seems to be another extreme: a totalization of *fallenness*, where discourse (the present *ecstasis*) is no longer grounded in one's personal attunement (the past *ecstasis*) or in one's authentic understanding (the future *ecstasis*). Postmodernists emphasize the role of the social order in constituting the self, or at least one's sense of self. Thus, in Heideggerian terms, they would affirm one's having fallen under the spell of "the they," without leaving room for such falling to represent a genuine relationship either to one's own past or to one's authentic future. If the sociobiologist sees the human being as just a disposable container for DNA, then the poststructuralist has a tendency to see the human being as just a disposable carrier of the grand narrative. Either way, there is a primacy of the code over the code carrier. And let's not leave out the shortcomings of the human potential movement: one might say that the "shadow" of the humanistic movement was its own totalization of Heidegger's third temporal horizon, *possibility*, over and against the obligations of the past and present. With Heidegger, individuals are understood as thrown projects or situated freedoms: there is a dialectic between the existential past and the existential future, between determinism and indeterminacy, between necessity and possibility, between facticity and existence.

[2] "*Facticity*' is the designation we will use for the character of the being of 'our' 'own' Dasein. More precisely, this expression means: *in each case* 'this' Dasein in its being there *for a while at the particular time*" (Heidegger, 1923/1999, p. 5). Heidegger was emphasizing here the particular "mineness" of one's being, as well as the finitude and duration of one's "finding oneself" situated. Hence, "there is a factivity of the experience of myself and the world. It seems that all knowledge rests on a constitution that is particular to me" (Merleau-Ponty, 1995/2003, p. 22).

[3] In *Being and Time,* Heidegger (1927/1962) made some remarkable pronouncements regarding the very nature of listening, of hearing, of being open to oneself and to others, and eventually, of hearkening. He wrote:

"Listening to ... is Dasein's existential way of Being-open as Being-with for Others. Indeed, hearing constitutes the primary and authentic way in which Dasein is open for its ownmost potentiality-for-Being—as in hearing the voice of the friend whom every Dasein carries with it. ... Being-with develops in listening to one another, which can be done in several possible ways: following, going along with, and the privative modes of not-hearing, resisting, defying, and turning away. It is on the basis of this potentiality for hearing, which is existentially primary, that anything like *hearkening* [*Horchen*] becomes possible. (pp 206–207)

Hearkening is a deeper kind of listening, in which one can even listen in silence. Heidegger (1927/1962) said that in the hearkening that comes from dwelling-with the Other, one is able to

provide [patients] with the opportunity to revise their stories in such a way that these will be more in line with what they want" (p. 45). What these therapists may be forgetting, however, is that what their patients want is a happier life, not just a happier story; they want their day to day experience to be free from anxiety, gloom, fear, etc.—and simply changing the way one talks about one's experience does not necessarily change the experience that exists in the first place. However, some postmodern thinkers seem to believe that what exists in the first place, so to speak, is the story.

In this particular variety of postmodern practice, the story that the client comes in with is treated as a myth: the narrative therapist, according to Parry and Doan (1994), is "a catalyst in the deconstruction of clients' or families' mythology" (p. 45). This is a far cry from the client-centered therapy where one learns to dwell in the client's words, to allow the words of the client to open up his or her world to the therapist. The Rogerian reverence for the client's words is replaced in postmodern therapy with a skepticism towards the clients own words—and, more alarming, with respect to their lived experience. Equally distinctive of this approach is the fact that the client is viewed less as an agent, as the author of his or her own story, and more as the passive victim of language games. If existential therapists try to teach their clients "I am what I choose to be," narrative therapists attempt to persuade their clients "I am the way I've been influenced to think I am" (Parry & Doan, 1994, p. 53). Postmodern therapists now deconstruct and revision the client's story, assuming that to not provide the client with a new and better story, is "to leave the clients in a state of 'psychological free fall.' Alternately stated, it is to leave them outside a story" (Parry & Doan, 1994, p. 45)—as if that were the worst thing imaginable! I use these quotations to demonstrate that I am not exaggerating the case, when I say that the postmodern therapist places stories, rather than experiences, at the center of ther-

---

experience something of who the other person is, through one's mode of attunement to him. In psychotherapy and psychological research, as well as in everyday life, this hearkening itself requires a sensitivity to one's own attunement (in this case, an attunement to the Other) as well as a sensitivity to the attunement of Others. When listening to a patient, or reading qualitative data, this sensitivity requires a bracketing of one's own first person feelings in similar situations, so that one can leave one's capacity for feeling available as a mode of attunement to the mode of Being-in revealed in the data. One's own subjective processes thus become instruments of one's perception of others. Hence, one can only truly understand the Other when one has been able to feel or suffer with the Other. One is not reminded of one's own suffering; this can come later. But for now, the individual "suffers with" as he bears witness to the Other. One might even become attuned to a suffering that lies just below the surface of the Other's expression, somewhere just out of his reach. But the person feels it, senses its presence, and knows that it is there. It is not revealed in what is said [explicitly] in the talk, but rather in what one understands that the talk is about. Such understanding requires moments of shared attunement that occur quite spontaneously, and which can only be cultivated, but never made to happen in the researcher's experience. In *Being-with-one-another understandingly*, one does not revert to one's own inner world; one remains curious and attentive to the Others' inner world, which is now a shared world.

apy. (Gergen & Gergen, 1998, offered a nicely dialogical model of postmodern thinking regarding the relationship of self to narrative—one with a more sophisticated philosophical foundation than one finds in some of the other representatives, such as the ones I have critiqued here.)

The dilemma here is that, after offering the patient a different story from the one he came in with—that is, a better, more coherent, more aesthetically pleasing (and maybe even self-congratulatory from the point of view of the patient) story—the therapy terminates. The woman mentioned earlier goes home, and she realizes her life is filled with the same dread, the same confusions. The new narrative wears off, as the old experience returns.

The dividing line between phenomenological psychology and postmodern psychology seems to have something to do with whether one abides by a primacy of experience or a primacy of language.[4] Merleau-Ponty (1945/1962) succinctly designated the problem faced by psychologists when he said that experience is, for the most part, lived, rather than known. Postmodern psychologists prefer, it seems, to beg this distinction and focus instead on what is spoken. My concern is that, once the chain of signifiers becomes dislocated from its foundation in experience, therapists end up with no objective reference point of which they can speak, or even allude to—and therefore no longer a concern on the part of the psychologist with whether the reality described by one story or another hits the mark, because the mark is now whatever story sounds best. This has been characterized by Bruner (1983, 1990) as a shift from a correspondence criterion for truth, to a coherence criterion. There has also been talk of an alternative pragmatic criterion for truth, and I believe it is this kind of utilitarian notion that "truth is whatever works for you" that has led to the current crisis in philosophical psychology (see Spence, 1982, pp. 275ff for a thoroughgoing critique of this position).

---

[4]I am deliberately remaining at a simple level, because my aim is to contrast the center of gravity of each of these movements—and postmodernism would caution against the very idea of centering (as opposed to decentering) characterizations! In fact, the relationship of phenomenology to postmodern thought is much more complicated, indeed, to the point where it can be asserted that one can "locate the beginning of philosophical postmodernism in Husserl" (Madison, 1988, p. xiii). "The history of the phenomenological movement," continued Madison, "is the history of the progressive attempt to eradicate the traces within it of … the metaphysical ghosts that continue to haunt our discourse, the house of being, as Heidegger called it." The underlying and more serious point of poststructuralism is to raise the question of what is the ultimate referent in discourse. As people like Lacan and Derrida have pointed out, there is only the myth of a transcendental signified; for postmodern thinkers, there are in fact only signifiers functioning in the structural role of the signified (Terry Pulver, personal communication). Psychologists such as Parry and Doan (1994), whose practical work consists of a narrative reframing of their clients' experiences, end up invoking theoretical systems with which their own work only bears a facile relationship.

II

I turn now to some methodological considerations for humanistic psychology in the wake of postmodernism. Because the intent here is to stimulate reflection (and perhaps motivate future submissions!) on the part of *The Humanistic Psychologist* readers, I do not presume to present a finished product but rather some questions that can be asked in the light of postmodern challenges. I represent humanistic psychology here with reference to its foundation in phenomenology.

Phenomenological research is oriented towards essences—or "unities of sense"—that become apparent when one runs through a plurality of instances of a particular experience in one's consciousness (Husserl, 1948/1973, pp 340–344). People's understanding of *meanings*, as well as *unities* or *wholes*, has been transformed in this past century, first by humanistic psychology and more recently by postmodern thought. Humanistic psychologists have turned their attention away from meaning as a content of consciousness, toward an appreciation of meaning as an activity of consciousness. Experience taken as a whole is not thought of as something static, but as something that unfolds in a process of becoming. Furthermore, the whole is not to be circumscribed by the boundaries of one's own body, but rather is understood to include those transpersonal realms that are invoked within one's own experience. Postmodern thinkers have helped to make people aware that meanings consist of "texts," through which individuals inscribe themselves in the world, and that the act of inscription, like the act of reading, is not simply the recording of an already existing meaning, but rather is itself a kind of birth of meaning. As Merleau-Ponty (1945/1962) observed, language does not express thought; rather, it accomplishes thought. With regard to wholes (including *gestalts*) postmodern thinkers are wary, and prefer to allow for disunities; the search for essences, structures, and identities is seen as serving a political establishment of norms that is intolerant of individual and cultural differences. The concept of *wholeness* must therefore be tempered to embrace rather than to exclude the accidental, the variable, or the abnormal. Postmodern thinkers (such as Derrida and Lacan) seem to have moved away from phenomenology as a method because they have been put off by the Husserlian search for essences or unities and instead prefer to speak of differences or "disunities." It was, nonetheless, the phenomenologist Sartre (1943/1956) who pointed out that one need not be deterred by such difficulties as indefinable or inhomogeneous objects of investigation:

> This is because there can be descriptions which do not aim at the essence but at the existent itself in its particularity. To be sure, I could not describe a freedom which would be common to both the Other and myself; I could not therefore contemplate an essence of freedom ... actually the question is of *my* freedom. Similarly when I described consciousness, I could not discuss a nature common to certain individuals but only *my* particular consciousness, which like my freedom is beyond essence. (p. 438)

If postmodern thinkers have a tendency of wanting to abandon method (or at least epistemology) altogether in view of a multiverse of narratives irreducible to any knowable essence, phenomenologists like Sartre still offer hope by suggesting and demonstrating that a diversity or heterogeneity of individual experience is no deterrent to developing a methodology for a psychological science. The new methodology will be a study precisely of human variance, rather than an effort to control or otherwise eliminate variance. This means there will be less concern with making claims for external validity, and thus a change in attitude toward the conventional ideal of randomness in sampling procedures. People will see a shift away from nomothetic studies, toward the idiographic (see, for example, Hoskins, 2001, 2002). And even if meaning is to be found in the particularities of individual experience rather than in the universalities or typicalities sought by modern scientists, a phenomenological method nonetheless turns out to be well suited to our purpose.

Where does this leave one, then, with regard to establishing the foundations for a program of research? There are three basic questions that must be addressed by any methodology, and I attempt here to sketch a tentative approach[5] for the new human study by addressing these questions: First, what kinds of questions shall researchers pose? Second, what kinds of data shall researchers collect and interrogate? Third, what kinds of knowledge (or formulations of "truth") will result?

QUESTIONS IN A CONTEXT OF DIVERSITY AND CHANGE

In the questions that one poses one will be addressing oneself to the idiosyncrasies of ever changing human realities. Having transcended the modern preoccupation with universals and essences, one can follow one's interests into the realm of the individual and the accidental where intentionalities and contingencies intertwine to coconstitute human existence. One can simply think of individual essences as what remains the same in one's perception of someone or something through a series of adumbrations—rather than as what remains the same in the individual.

If the contribution of humanistic psychology within the research tradition of modern psychology has been its willingness to affirm the creative potential of humanity, then the contribution of postmodern thought is its reminder that whatever one strives to create, one must do so without being able to claim any universality or permanence to our creation. The new questions for psychological inquiry thus become: "How do human beings create reality in a time when reality appears to be

---

[5]I employ the term *approach* here with great indebtedness to Amedeo Giorgi, whose teaching and writing serves as rich source and context for the more circumscribed issues being addressed here. See Giorgi (1970) for a poignant and compelling articulation of the meaning of *approach* within the scientific enterprise in general and within psychology in particular. In this text, Giorgi articulates a radically new paradigm for psychology, influenced by Merleau-Ponty's (1942/1963) notion of *structure*.

more and more transient?" and "To what extent can any one individual's creations be taken as reflective of 'humanity itself'?" These lead to a third question: "What kinds of 'realities' (actual or virtual) are created by humanity?" These questions are not of the kind that one would normally develop a methodology to address; they are reflective questions of a foundational nature that one might pose in the wake of inquiries already undertaken. It will be important, then, to maintain a distinction between questions of an overarching nature that provide a context as well as an inspiration for research, and questions of a more circumscribed nature that can be addressed more directly using qualitative or quantitative methods.

Researchers typically address general questions by "operationalizing" the questions into observable events and finding adequate means of sampling the target population. With "humanity" itself as the population of interest, there is an immediate problem with respect to the external validity of any research investigation. The challenge will be for methodologists to design studies that reflect "humanity" without being either reductionistic or totalizing, and this will require some new thinking with regard to what constitutes "data" and how one arrives at "results."

DATA AS A NARRATIVE CONSTRUCT

It was R. D. Laing (1967) who suggested referring to the subject matter of psychology as *capta* rather than *data* because "the 'data' (given) of research are not so much given as *taken* out of a constantly elusive matrix of happenings" (p. 62). What he acknowledged here are the peculiar natures of the process and content of psychology. As a *logos*, psychology selectively illuminates its subject matter, and in effect its findings are captured by a creative mind rather than merely recorded on a blank slate. Moreover, the constantly elusive matrix that forms the subject matter of psychology is an ever-changing nexus or totality (Dilthey, 1894/1977, called it a *Zusammenhang*) that includes the presence of the psychologist. For postmodern psychologists, this matrix is understood to be a system of discourse that is elusive only to the extent that it is essentially idiosyncratic. Each moment of psychological insight represents a happening that takes place between an instance of human conduct and the narrative context that is the researcher's presence.

The implication is that psychologists need no longer search for objective truths or feel obliged to make claims that their knowledge is based on fact. In a revitalized humanistic research paradigm, theorists will acknowledge that their starting point is not an accumulation of bare facts, but rather an act of positing by which they coconstitute their very sense of what it is they are studying. As Polkinghorne (1991) observed,

> each language system has its own particular way of distorting, filtering, and constructing experience … . Each language system is to be recognized and honored as one among the many systems by which order can be constructed in experience. …

Rather than reproductions of clear pictures of the real as it is in itself, human experience consists of meaningful interpretations of the real (see also Polkinghorne, 1988).

It may be even more appropriate to say that human experience consists of meaningful interpretations that *are* the real. If psychological reality is the subject matter, then it is already a narrative reality. What is true in everyday life is every bit as true for researchers: they respond not to "objective" qualities of the subject matter but to qualities that are a function of one's perspective on our subject matter

ANALYSIS OF DATA: TOWARD AN EPISTEMOLOGY FOR HUMANISTIC RESEARCH

More than a century ago, Dilthey (1894/1977) remarked that in understanding one draws on all of the powers of the psyche: sensing, judging, remembering, imagining, intuiting, feeling, and thinking. How ironic, then, that when empirical psychologists go to the encounter with their subject matter, they bring with them a truncated understanding whose claim to fame is its reliance on sense data and calculative thinking, to the exclusion of other modes of understanding such as feeling, intuiting, and imagining. In aspiring to be scientific, psychologists have adamantly based their theories on observation, and yet they have restricted themselves to essentially one mode of observation: sensation. Unfortunately, they have forsaken the very modes of perception that might conceivably offer them the most direct and faithful access to their subject.

If a methodology for humanistic research would raise questions about the meanings of consciousness, conduct, and culture in a context of diversity and change, then the methods employed would be predicated on a sensitivity to meanings requiring some form of direct existential contact between the researcher and the phenomenon. Such contact could be achieved by establishing an empathic relationship with the data. Human science researchers can take as data, and thereby submit to their powers of understanding, just about any form of human expression: verbal testimony, written protocols, observed behavior, gestures, drawings, art works, cultural artifacts, and media presentations. To be sure, these data must be perceived by the senses in some way or another for them to be understood. But understanding exceeds the powers of sensation in the same way that psychological meaning transcends the purely material events occurring in the brain while experience takes place. Material events of behavior and the sensations that register them in the brain of the researcher are merely superficial occurrences. Meaning is an event that reflects what one might call the depths of the psyche. It is what inspired Freud (see especially Freud, 1905/1963, pp. 59–61) to invent his depth psychology, which sought the meaning, or intent of, the symptom over and above its material cause.

What is important to bear in mind is that the relationship between a behavior and its meaning or intent is not a simple correspondence, such as might be understood to exist between a material object and its weight. This is what has led philosophers of science to contrast narrative truth with historical truth, and to speak of "interpretation as an artistic and pragmatic creation that is always oriented toward the future" (Spence, 1982, p. 287). If one's understanding of behavior, like behavior itself, is always oriented toward the future, then one must not look back; perhaps it is the case that one cannot look back (that is, to justify or ground one's assertions in their relationship to historical fact). This, of course, raises a problem with respect to the validation of our findings. To simply ask for a good story leaves one open to too many inadequacies: using narrative fit alone as a criterion for adequacy, one discovers that there are numerous plausible accounts that might never be proven. Psychoanalytic therapy, however, does not require that the analyst's reconstruction of a childhood event be objectively confirmed for it to have subjective truth value—that is, pragmatic value for the present and future of the patient. Feyerabend (1975) took this position to the extreme, suggesting

> once it has been realized that close empirical fit is no virtue and that it must be relaxed in times of change, then style, elegance of expression, simplicity of presentation, tension of plot and narrative, and seductiveness of content become important features of our knowledge.

In practice, I believe that aesthetic criteria for validity will not suffice and that humanistic psychologists needs to strive for coherence and correspondence, even if of a limited nature, and that perhaps they should consider a third term that embraces both of these criteria. The term connectedness might serve to suggest the need for description to be adequately grounded in evidence (albeit not a simple self-evidence), but expressed in a way that preserves the *Zusammenhang* or *gestalt* of human experience. Furthermore, it suggests the need for understanding to be connected to the future, in the Heideggerian sense of a "projection" into possibility (1927/1962, p. 185). That is, our formulations of truth should facilitate our journey through life.

In the end, the value of research will depend on its ability to help ourselves to gain insight into the vicissitudes of human experience. Further investigations from other viewpoints may then supplement and possibly even radically de-center what remains a forever-limited knowledge of human life.

REFERENCES

Berger, P. L., & Luckmann, T. (1966). *The social construction of reality: A treatise on the sociology of knowledge.* New York: Doubleday.

Bruner, J. S. (1983, August). *Conceptual and narrative modes of thought.* Paper presented at the 92nd Annual Convention of the American Psychological Association, Toronto, Canada.

Bruner, J. S. (1990). *Acts of meaning.* Cambridge, MA: Harvard University Press.

Churchill, S. D. (2002). Stories of experience and the experience of stories: Narrative psychology, phenomenology, and the postmodern challenge. *Constructivism and the Human Sciences, 7,* 81–93.

Derrida, J. (1973). *Speech and phenomena* (D. Allison, Trans.). Evanston, IL: Northwestern University Press. (Original work published 1967)

Derrida, J. (1976). *Of grammatology* (G. C. Spivak, Trans.). Baltimore: Johns Hopkins University Press. (Original work published 1967)

Dilthey, W. (1977). Ideas concerning a descriptive and analytical psychology (1894). (R. M. Zaner, Trans.). In W. Dilthey (Ed.), *Descriptive psychology and historical understanding* (pp. 23–120). The Hague: Martinus Nijhoff. (Original work published, 1924)

Feyerabend, X. (1975). *Against method: Outline of an anarchistic theory of knowledge.* London: Redwood Barn..

Foucault, M. (1976). *The archaeology of knowledge* (A. M. Sheridan, Trans.). New York: Harper Colophon. (Original work published 1969)

Foucault, M. (1980). *Power and knowledge* (C. Gordon, L. Marshall, J. Mepham, & K. Soper, Trans.). New York: Pantheon.

Freud, S. (1963). *Dora: A fragment of an analysis* (P. Rieff, Ed.). New York: Collier. (Original work published 1905)

Gergen, K. J. (1991). *The saturated self: Dilemmas of identity in contemporary life.* New York: Basic Books.

Gergen, K. J., & Gergen, M. M. (1998). Narrative and the self as relationship. *Advances in Experimental Social Psychology, 21,* 17–56.

Giorgi, A. (1970). *Psychology as a human science: A phenomenologically-based approach.* New York: Harper & Row.

Heidegger, M. (1956). The way back into the ground of metaphysics (W. Kaufman, Trans.). In W. Kaufmann (Ed.), *Existentialism from Dostoevsky to Sartre* (pp. 206–221). New York: Random House. (Original work published 1949)

Heidegger, M. (1962). *Being and time* (J. MacQuarrie & E. Robinson, Trans.). New York: Harper & Row. (Original work published 1927)

Heidegger, M. (1999). *Ontology—The hermeneutics of facticity* (J. van Buren, Trans.). Bloomington: Indiana University Press. (Lecture course from the summer semester of 1923, Freiburg. *Gesamtausgabe* vol. 63, 1988)

Heidegger, M. (2005). *Introduction to phenomenological research* (D. O. Dahlstrom, Trans.). Bloomington: Indiana University Press. (Lecture course from the winter semester of 1923–1924, Marburg. *Gesamtausgabe* vol. 17, 1994)

Hoskins, M. L. (2001). True grit and the new frontier: Cultivating new ground for psychological research. *Qualitative Inquiry, 7,* 659–675.

Hoskins, M. L. (2002). Towards new methodologies for constructivist research: Synthesizing knowledges for relational inquiries. In J. D. Raskin & S. K. Bridges (Eds.), *Studies in meaning: Exploring constructivist psychology* (pp. 225–244). New York: Pace University Press.

Husserl, E. (1973). *Experience and judgment* (J. S. Churchill & I. Ameriks, Trans.). Evanston, IL: Northwestern University Press. (Original work published 1948)

Laing, R. D. (1967). *The politics of experience.* New York: Ballantine.

Madison , G. B. (1988). *The hermeneutics of postmodernity: Figures and themes.* Bloomington: Indiana University Press.

Merleau-Ponty, M. (1962). *Phenomenology of perception* (C. Smith, Trans.). London: Routledge & Kegan Paul. (Original work published 1945)

Merleau-Ponty, M. (2003). *Nature: Course notes from the College de France* (P. Vollier, Trans.). Evanston, IL: Northwestern University Press. (Original work published 1995)

Parry, A., & Doan, R. E. (1994). *Story re-visions: Narrative therapy in the postmodern world.* New York: Guilford Press.

Polkinghorne, D. (1988). *Narrative knowing and the human sciences.* Albany, NY: SUNY Press.

Polkinghorne, D. (1991). *Postmodern epistemology of practice.* Unpublished manuscript, University of Southern California, Los Angeles.

Sartre, J.-P. (1956). *Being and nothingness: A phenomenological essay on ontology* (H. Barnes, Trans.). New York: Philosophical Library. (Original work published 1943)

Spence, D. P. (1982). *Narrative truth and historical truth: Meaning and interpretation in psychoanalysis.* New York: Norton.

ACKNOWLEDGMENTS

Much of this article was incorporated into the Division 32 Presidential Address *Humanistic Psychologies: Forward We Go Into the 21st Century* presented at the 113th Annual Convention of the American Psychological Association, August 20, 2005. (An earlier version of portions of this article was presented in K. Gergen [Chair], *The Place of Value in a Psychology Without Foundations*, Symposium presented at the 109th Annual Convention of the American Psychological Association, San Francisco, August 27, 2001.

AUTHOR NOTE

Scott D. Churchill, PhD is Professor and Graduate Program Director in the Department of Psychology at the University of Dallas. He is currently a Fellow of the APA, serving as Division 32 President and Associate Editor for *The Humanistic Psychologist,* as well as Secretary–Treasurer of the Society for Theoretical and Philosophical Psychology (Division 24). He served as Editor of *Methods: A Journal for Human Science* from 1989 to 2003. His recent publications include entries in the APA's *Encyclopedia of Psychology*; chapters in *The Handbook of Humanistic Psychology,* and in Ron Valle's *Phenomenological Inquiry: Existential and Transpersonal Dimensions;* as well as articles in *The Humanistic Psychologist, Constructivism in the Human Sciences, Journal of Phenomenological Psychology, Journal of Theoretical and Philosophical Psychology, Qualitative Research in Psychology, The Psychotherapy Patient,* and *Somatics.* He is currectly senior film critic for *Irving Community Television Network* and a volunteer "Roots and Shoots" coordinator for the Jane Goodall Institute.

THE HUMANISTIC PSYCHOLOGIST, *33*(4), 335
Copyright © 2005, Lawrence Erlbaum Associates, Inc.

ACKNOWLEDGMENTS

Volume 32, Number 4 of *The Humanistic Psychologist* (the 2004 *Methods* Issue) was guest edited by Rosemarie Anderson of The Institute for Transpersonal Psychology. *The Humanistic Psychologist* regrets that Darby Publishing did not put her name on the cover as a special guest editor. The issue was superb and the work she did outstanding. She deserved this acknowledgment.

Likewise, Volume 32, Number 2 and Volume 31, Number 4 (the 2003 *Methods* Issue) were both edited by Scott D. Churchill.

T - #0159 - 270225 - C0 - 229/152/5 - PB - 9780805894066 - Gloss Lamination